THE
NBA
STORY

How the Sports League Slam-Dunked Its
Way into a Global Business Powerhouse

© 2020 HarperCollins Leadership

Published by HarperCollins Leadership, an imprint of HarperCollins Focus LLC.

Published in association with Kevin Anderson & Associates: https://www.ka-writing.com/.

Book design by Aubrey Khan, Neuwirth & Associates.

ISBN 978-1-4002-1886-8 (eBook)
ISBN 978-1-4002-1885-1 (HC)

Library of Congress Control Number: 2020931298

Printed in the United States of America
20 21 22 23 LSC 10 9 8 7 6 5 4 3 2 1

CONTENTS

ACKNOWLEDGMENTS

I would like to thank Joe Newman, cofounder of the ABA; Joanne Lannin, author and expert on women's basketball including the ABA; and the NBA's Senior VP of International Basketball Operations Kim Bohuny, for taking the time to be interviewed for the book. I would also like to thank Eric Mintzer for his research, writing, and assistance throughout, and my wife, Carol, for her support. An additional thank you goes out to HarperCollins and Kevin Anderson and Associates for allowing me to write about the NBA, a business I've supported for many years.

—Rich

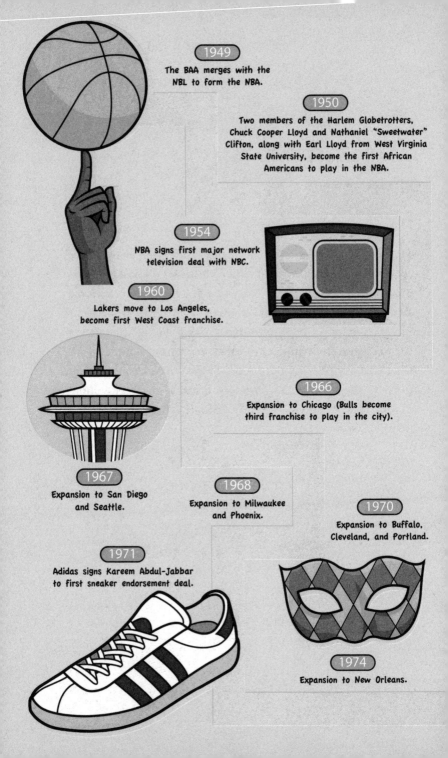

1949
The BAA merges with the NBL to form the NBA.

1950
Two members of the Harlem Globetrotters, Chuck Cooper Lloyd and Nathaniel "Sweetwater" Clifton, along with Earl Lloyd from West Virginia State University, become the first African Americans to play in the NBA.

1954
NBA signs first major network television deal with NBC.

1960
Lakers move to Los Angeles, become first West Coast franchise.

1966
Expansion to Chicago (Bulls become third franchise to play in the city).

1967
Expansion to San Diego and Seattle.

1968
Expansion to Milwaukee and Phoenix.

1970
Expansion to Buffalo, Cleveland, and Portland.

1971
Adidas signs Kareem Abdul-Jabbar to first sneaker endorsement deal.

1974
Expansion to New Orleans.

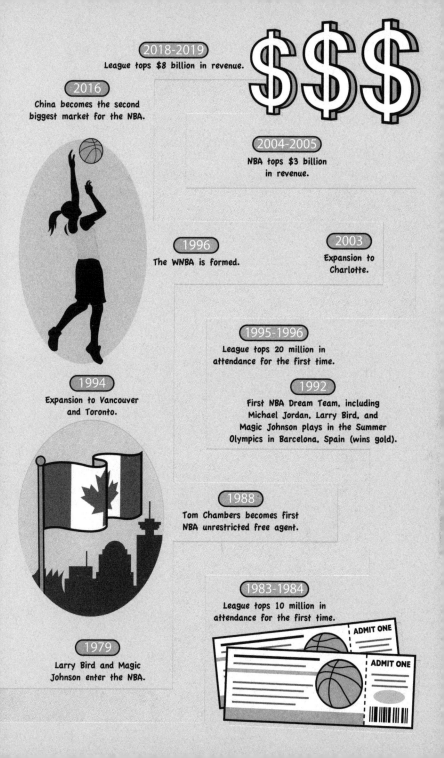

2018-2019
League tops $8 billion in revenue.

2016
China becomes the second biggest market for the NBA.

2004-2005
NBA tops $3 billion in revenue.

1996
The WNBA is formed.

2003
Expansion to Charlotte.

1995-1996
League tops 20 million in attendance for the first time.

1994
Expansion to Vancouver and Toronto.

1992
First NBA Dream Team, including Michael Jordan, Larry Bird, and Magic Johnson plays in the Summer Olympics in Barcelona, Spain (wins gold).

1988
Tom Chambers becomes first NBA unrestricted free agent.

1983-1984
League tops 10 million in attendance for the first time.

1979
Larry Bird and Magic Johnson enter the NBA.

ADMIT ONE

ADMIT ONE

L ittle did college professor James Naismith know that the game he invented in 1891, which centered around two teams trying to throw a ball into a peach basket—in an attempt to keep his students occupied indoors during inclement weather—would someday become an international phenomenon played in over 100 countries. Just over forty-five years after Naismith tossed the first jump ball in the air, the NBA was founded and has, some seventy plus years later, emerged as the premiere basketball league in the world, amongst highly competitive leagues in Europe, Asia, Africa, and South America. The league features international players and has a diverse fan base that spans the globe.

The NBA is also a multibillion-dollar business generating wealth from sources that include ticket sales, merchandising, and television revenue. A host of other leagues have since been formed by the NBA to provide inclusion and greater diversity for the great game of basketball. Today's NBA also reaches out and touches young athletes and fans with community outreach and training and development programs worldwide.

But the league was not always the shining example of incredible business success it is today. In the early years, the NBA was faced with teams folding, fans getting bored, and disenchanted players who wanted some sense of financial stability. Like many startup businesses, there were numerous challenges and off-the-court pivots that would need to be made before the league would begin what has become a meteoric rise.

In the pages that follow, we will take a look at the story of the NBA, recounting the on-court and off-court activities that built the NBA into an international phenomenon.

"Some people
want it to happen,
some wish it to happen,
others make it happen."

—MICHAEL JORDAN

CHAPTER ONE

THE FOUNDING AND STARTUP YEARS

The fast-paced excitement of today's NBA, with mega popular multimillion-dollar athletes and a multibillion-dollar television deal, started out, like most businesses, on a wing and a prayer. The hope was that such a competitive sport could bring some excitement and joy to a nation that had just played an integral part in World War II. Soldiers were back home, families were moving to the suburbs, and the time was right to grow a professional indoor, winter sports league that would not conflict with the nation's beloved summer pastime, baseball. It was a sport that had grown organically, starting as a game played in school gymnasiums, playgrounds, and YMCAs, then graduated to high school and college teams. It had already gone professional, but the NBA was going to improve upon the business of basketball as never seen before.

The National Basketball Association was the result of a business merger. It took place initially in 1946 when two rival men's basketball leagues, both struggling for different reasons, merged, the National Basketball League (NBL) and the Basketball Association of America (BAA). Together they remained a larger version of the BAA for three seasons before being officially billed as the National Basketball Association (NBA) in 1949. However, NBA statistics include those final three BAA seasons and the 1946 merger is widely considered the league's starting point.

Unlike many businesses, the NBA was conceived as, and remains, an entirely independent and fully self-managed organizational body (a limited corporation) whose members, the teams, are franchises operating as businesses that are independently owned. In 1946, each team paid a franchise fee of $10,000. Today, a new team entering the NBA would pay upward of $300 million.

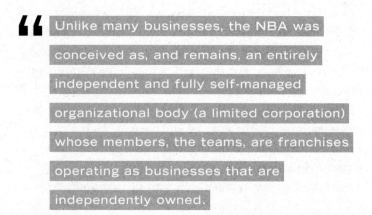

" Unlike many businesses, the NBA was conceived as, and remains, an entirely independent and fully self-managed organizational body (a limited corporation) whose members, the teams, are franchises operating as businesses that are independently owned.

The league operated, and continues to operate, under a constitution and a set of bylaws that constitute a contract among the members of the association, who are the owners, now sometimes referred to as governors. These team owners worked out the details of the league constitution and bylaws.

The NBA Constitution spells out the governance structure of the league, including the rights and responsibilities of the team owners, the board of governors, and the commissioner. The NBA bylaws provide the framework for the operation of the league, which includes team and player requirements.

The league commissioner, known as the league president until 1967, would be elected by the owners. He was granted disciplinary power, dispute resolution authority, and decision-making authority, including the power to appoint other officers and committees. The owners, in conjunction with the initial league president, created the initial league rules, which were based, to a large degree, on the rules of the previous leagues and on those used in college basketball. It should also be noted that in the initial season, the NBA had a salary cap, which was eliminated after just one season and did not return for nearly forty years.

While the league was now in the startup phase, funded almost entirely by the franchise owners, issues arose almost immediately, which is not unusual following such a merger. The most notable concern was that while the leagues both offered the same product, professional men's basketball, they had radically different markets: small town and big city.

The National Basketball League, established in 1937, consisted primarily of Midwestern teams sponsored by some of the major corporations of the time, such as the Anderson Packers founded by the owners of a meat packing business in Anderson, Indiana, and the Akron Firestone Non-Skids, named for the Firestone Tire and Rubber Company, based in Akron, Ohio. The NBL teams played most of their games for small crowds in small venues. The Indianapolis Olympians, for example, played in the Hinkle Fieldhouse while the Fort Wayne Pistons actually played their home games in the North

Side High School gymnasium. Five of the teams in the current NBA trace their roots back to the NBL. What made the NBL worthy of the merger was that they had the more talented, better-known collegiate players, and college basketball had already gained notoriety with tournaments dating back to the 1920s.

Meanwhile, the Basketball Association of America featured teams in larger markets, which played at venues such as at Madison Square Garden, home to the New York Knicks, and the Boston Garden, home to the Celtics. The big markets were a plus, especially when it came to local marketing, at the expense of the teams, and drawing larger crowds, However, the caliber of play was not at the level of the NBL teams.

The plan was to have four of the more successful NBL franchises join the BAA to complete the merger and hopefully bring together the star players from smaller markets with the drawing power of the teams playing in major markets. This would mean people in New York City or Boston, for example, could see top young stars, (still well-known from their college days), even if they were not on the home teams.

Launching the Business

The new league unveiled their product in Canada on November 1, 1946. While the league was still technically the BAA, this is considered the first-ever NBA game and it was played between the New York Knicks and the Toronto Huskies in front of a crowd of 7,090 at Maple Leaf Garden. It was not a bad turnout considering Toronto was known as a "hockey town." Even the arena, Maple Leaf Arena, was named for the city's NHL team. Longtime sportswriter Sam Goldaper, covering the game, wrote that the game "bore little resemblance to the leaping, balletic version of today's NBA. That game was from a different era of low-scoring basketball, a time when hoops as a pro spectacle was just coming out of the dance halls. Players did not routinely double-pump or slam-dunk. The fact of the matter was that the players did not and could not jump very well. Nor was there a 24-second clock; teams had unlimited time to shoot. The jump shot was a radical notion, and those who took it defied the belief of many coaches that nothing but trouble occurred when a player left his feet for a shot."[1] The Knicks won the league opener 68–66.

Maurice Podoloff

The person responsible for bringing the two leagues together was Maurice Podoloff, a distinguished attorney who headed the BAA from its inception. Podoloff was also president of the American Hockey League and founder of the New Haven Arena which he opened in the mid-1920s with his brothers. He was more knowledgeable in law and real estate than he was in sports. However, being a good negotiator served him well while dealing with the differing personalities of the team owners. Following the merger, Podoloff would serve as president of the new league which would include seventeen teams in three divisions. The season would run from October through March with each team having an awkward schedule which had teams playing between sixty-two and sixty-eight games, followed by playoffs in April.

Podoloff would spend seventeen years at the helm of the NBA, constantly supporting team owners in their quest to stay financially solvent. He introduced the college draft in 1947 which would bring new talent into the league every year and secured the league's first television deals for the NBA, first in 1953 with the DuMont Network for one season and then a long-term deal starting in 1954 with NBC.

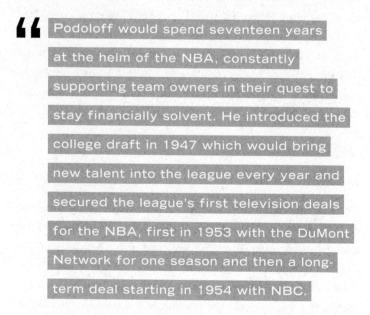

Podoloff would spend seventeen years at the helm of the NBA, constantly supporting team owners in their quest to stay financially solvent. He introduced the college draft in 1947 which would bring new talent into the league every year and secured the league's first television deals for the NBA, first in 1953 with the DuMont Network for one season and then a long-term deal starting in 1954 with NBC.

Startup Years

Since the NBA was not a totally new business, it had an established product with professional men's basketball, there was already a small but steady fan base. The franchises maintained most of their players, some of whom had already developed a local following. League offices were maintained by a small staff in New York City while the owners maintained their franchise offices and remained enthusiastic during the early years, well-aware that they still held the purse strings, and that if their enthusiasm weaned they could exchanges players, sell the team, look to relocate or dissolve the franchise entirely.

College basketball provided the most significant competition to the league in the early years. However, the popularity of the college game also worked in favor of the league by providing talent once Podoloff initiated the college draft. This attracted fans who had read about college stars to see if they were as good as the rave reviews in the sports pages.

Among the NBA players who were already well known from their college days and had established themselves as stars in their local markets were Dolph Schayes, Neil Johnston, Bob Pettit, and Paul Arizin. While they all excelled in the early years of the league, one additional player was noteworthy for his impact on the sport and that was George Mikan. He played for the BAA, and then the NBA, for the Minneapolis Lakers. Mikan was the NBA's first big man, at 6'10", 245 pounds, and the first *must-see* superstar. He not only led his team to five titles, but he drew fans wherever the Lakers played. Mikan also created the drill for big men to practice shooting (known as the Mikan Drill) and was the impetus for several of the league's rule changes.

Despite the presence of Mikan and a favorable environment for the league, overall ticket sales remained low, particularly in the small markets, and there were no major television deals to drive revenue and promote the league during those first few seasons. In fact, college doubleheaders were still bigger draws than NBA games. Several NBA teams had difficulty scheduling their home games around ice hockey, boxing, and other events at some of the major arenas.

The league was almost entirely dependent on ticket sales as a source of revenue and Podoloff, along with the team owners, were constantly trying to market the product. To help publicize the new league, Podoloff hired J. Walter Kennedy, who was well known within the sports media establishment, having served as the publicity director for the Harlem Globetrotters on their national and international tours.

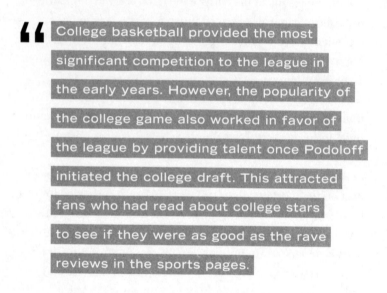

College basketball provided the most significant competition to the league in the early years. However, the popularity of the college game also worked in favor of the league by providing talent once Podoloff initiated the college draft. This attracted fans who had read about college stars to see if they were as good as the rave reviews in the sports pages.

Movement and Contraction

In hopes of increasing attendance, several team owners moved their franchises to new markets, some making several moves before finding a more permanent home. Teams such as the Tri-City Blackhawks would move to Milwaukee in 1951 in hopes of gaining more attendance. When that didn't happen, they moved to St. Louis in 1955 where they would play for thirteen years before moving to Atlanta, where they remain today. The Fort Wayne Pistons would leave the high school gymnasium for an arena in Detroit in 1957; they too have stayed put. Other teams would move to larger markets, where they would either thrive or move again, such as the Rochester Royals who, due to lack of profitability, started making their way across the country, first to Cincinnati, then to Kansas City-Omaha and finally to Sacramento, where they were anointed "Kings."

In some cases, owners found a new market that was eager to watch professional basketball, so they moved their teams, while in other cases, owners failed miserably. Several disgruntled team owners tried to move their teams, but could not secure a profitable city with an arena in which to play. It was (and still is) also quite difficult to sell a franchise in a fledgling young business. As a result, some team owners threw in the towel early on, deciding that it was better to take smaller losses rather than hanging onto a sinking ship in a struggling league. Contraction within the NBA dropped the league from the original seventeen teams down to ten by the second season (eleven with the addition of the Baltimore Bullets). The league was down to just eight teams by the start of the 1955–56 season. It wouldn't be until 1970, some twenty-one years later, that the NBA would return to the seventeen-team league at which they started.

Innovation Saves the NBA

Maurice Podoloff, an astute businessman, provided the league with a strong business plan, built in part on the wisdom of notable management consultant Peter Drucker, who emphasized the need to recognize what the customer wants. In this case, the customers were the fans, and they wanted to see a fast-paced game between some of the country's finest athletes. With that in mind, Podoloff was still looking for suggestions to improve the fan experience.

Led by George Mikan, the new league was generating fan interest, as anticipated, plus the NBA was drawing additional crowds in the early years by having the Harlem Globetrotters as an opening act, largely thanks to J. Walter Kennedy. The Globetrotters, formed in 1926, were established worldwide as entertainers who would bring their remarkable mixed bag of basketball skills and comedic repartee to the court in a preliminary game before the NBA teams would tip-off. They were crowd-pleasers wherever they went, and the NBA was glad to have them bring more ticket holders into the arenas.

It's also worth mentioning that in 1950 two of the Globetrotters, Chuck Cooper Lloyd and Nathaniel "Sweetwater" Clifton, along with West Virginia State University star, Earl Lloyd, became the first three African Americans to play in the young league. Cooper debuted for the Celtics, Clifton for the Knicks, and Lloyd for the Washington Capitals.

■ UNEXPECTED BOOST

Not anticipated by the NBA, but also working in their favor, was a major college point-shaving scandal that rocked the sports world in 1951 involving teams in seventeen states, and many games, including playoff games. This caused cancellations of a number of college basketball doubleheaders that drew fans to some of the major arenas.

Yet the league still wasn't making money. The biggest problem the new league faced went beyond the location of franchises or scheduling home games in the major arenas. It also went beyond any competition from other sports. The league's problems were internal. The NBA was a new business without an exciting product. The games had become methodical and fans were simply bored. The lack of scoring was a huge problem. Teams would get a lead and then stall, holding onto the ball, killing as much time as they could while sending fans into a stupor. The only ways to get the ball back was for a player to foul someone on the opposing team and after they made free throws they would get possession, or they would need to get a rebound off a missed free throw. This resulted in turning the game into tedious free throw shooting contests.

In 1950, the league hit rock bottom when Fort Wayne defeated Minnesota in the lowest-scoring game in NBA history. The game, called the Fort Wayne Freeze by Eric Nadel (ironically) in his book called *The Night Wilt Scored 100: Tales from Basketball's Past*, was a situation in which the Fort Wayne Pistons were in Minneapolis to play the Lakers, who sported the league's brightest star George Mikan, and a twenty-nine-game winning streak. The Pistons had a plan, which was simply to stall by holding onto the basketball as long as possible. Writes Nadel, "The referees could do nothing to speed up the game and the fans were irate when the first half ended—even though the Lakers held a 13–11 lead. The Piston players had to surround their coach, Murray Mendenhall, from outraged fans on the way to the locker room." When the game ended with the Pistons winning by the score of 19–18, "Podoloff instructed the owners and coaches never to let that happen again," wrote Nadel.[2]

Innovation was sorely needed; clearly something had to be done to speed up the game. In 1954, with the game desperately in need of a shot in the arm the owner of the Syracuse Nationals, Danny Biasone, and his general manager, Leo Ferris, came up with an idea. A team in possession of the ball would have only 24 seconds in which to take a shot, otherwise the ball would be turned over to the other team. The owners voted in favor of utilizing what would be called the 24-second clock. Rarely does a rule change, or changing a product, show immediate results, but in this case, it made a world of difference. The first game played with the 24-second clock finished with a score of 98–95. The pace of the game changed significantly, and the fans loved it. Suddenly there was a quickness and an urgency to score. Players were running up court, throwing the ball around and no longer taking forever to take a shot. In short, NBA basketball as we know it today was born in 1954, and fans saw a radical difference in the sport. This one simple rule change initiated by Biasone and Ferris did nothing less than save the NBA.

Improvements

Like any forward-thinking business, the NBA looked at the trends established in the league and made changes to encourage or discourage what they felt would help improve the game draw of fans. Along with the 24-second clock, the NBA made a number of improvements to their product during the early years in the form of rule changes, some of which were initiated by the league's star player who used his size to, unintentionally, influence such adjustments. For example, the foul lanes were widened from six to twelve feet for the 1954–55 season, primarily because George Mikan could reach out and grab a missed free throw and simply put it in the basket. Mikan could also stand in front of the basket and swat away anything that appeared to be going in.

As a result of Mikan, the goal-tending role, which had been initiated in the National Collegiate Athletic Association (NCAA) a few years earlier, was also adopted by the NBL and then by the

NBA. Clearly all new businesses need to adjust as they move forward and the NBA adjusted their product as necessary.

The Players' Union

While the league suddenly had greater hope for survival with the introduction of the 24-second clock, and other new rules, the players had a number of off-court concerns.

According to NBA history, players had no per diem, no minimum wage, no health benefits, no pension plan, and the average player salary was roughly $8,000 in the early 1950s. Issues such as transportation from city to city were often challenging and players were frequently on their own when it came to getting a bus or train to the next game.[3]

The NBA players loved the game but were clearly, and vocally, frustrated by the league's inability to provide benefits. In 1954–55 season, with the league still in the formative years, and job security depending on the stability of each team, Bob Cousy (of the Boston Celtics) one of the league's premier players, decided it was time to unionize the players. Cousy knew he would need the support of other prominent players if he was going to make his plan work, so he reached out to the highest profile talent on other teams, such as Carl Braun of the New York Knicks, Dolph Schayes of the Syracuse Nationals, and Paul Arizin of the Philadelphia Warriors to help drum-up player support for the union. The plan worked and the National Basketball Players Association (NBPA) was formed. It was the first players' union in organized sports in the United States.[4]

After gathering several grievances of the players, Cousy took the list of concerns to Podoloff, who now officially served as league's first commissioner. Along with the team owners,

Podoloff put off the NBPA concerns for nearly two years until Cousy sought out a possible union affiliation with the AFL-CIO. This got Podoloff's attention, yet it still took some time before the league acted. Finally, several of the early player concerns were agreed upon by the owners and the players' union in 1957 including a seven dollar per diem, other reasonable traveling expenses, an increase in the playoff pool, and reasonable moving expenses for players traded during a season. Although the NBPA was making some headway, it would take several years before the owners began taking the union seriously. Frustrated by the owners' attitudes toward the union, Cousy turned the reins over to his Boston teammate Tom Heinsohn, who took on the issue of a player's pension, and also ran up against resistance from the owners.[5]

As the league was perched to move into the 1960s, players' grievances would continue to be a sticking point for owners. Yet, the league, after a long fourteen-year gestation period, was finally seeing the ascent they had hoped for, and some teams were now making money.

■ THE PROOF IS IN THE NUMBERS

Led by the Celtics topping 260,000 in attendance in the 1956–57 season (or 10,500+ per game) and the Knicks setting an attendance record of over 335,000 in the 1959–60 season (or 10,800 per game), the NBA was beginning to see the fruits of their startup years. League attendance had climbed from just over one million fans (roughly 3,000 per game) in the 1946–47 season to nearly 1.3 million fans in attendance during the 1959–60 season (or over 5,000 per game).[6]

"Basketball is a beautiful game when the five players on the court play with one heartbeat."

—DEAN SMITH

CHAPTER TWO

THE FIRST GREAT RIVALRY, EXPANSION, AND TV DEALS IN THE 1960S

The early years of the NBA were marked by the dichotomy of large and small markets, contraction, relocation, competition with college basketball, significant rule changes, and conflicts that still needed to be addressed, and resolved, between the team owners and players. By the start of the 1960s, at least one star player had been established on almost every franchise, and after some sluggish years, attendance climbed from just over 3,500 fans per game in the 1950–51 season to over 5,000 per game in the 1959–60 season.[1]

As the league proceeded into the 1960s, they had a flagship franchise leading the way. The Boston Celtics were the big market team driving the league forward, always among the top in attendance, and throughout the decade, they would become the most successful when it came to winning titles. Creating a flagship franchise in sports can be challenging. Unlike other franchise businesses, in which the product can be quite similar, if not the same, at all locations, the NBA product is driven by talent, and that can vary greatly from franchise to franchise. Nonetheless, most of the major markets were able to maintain growing fan interest despite results, which typically meant losing seasons.

Fortunately for the NBA, their flagship Celtics, led by Bill Russell, had something 300 miles away that was a major benefit to any professional sports league or association . . . a rivalry. The Philadelphia Warriors were not only a worthy opponent in a major market, but they featured the legendary Wilt (the Stilt) Chamberlain standing over seven feet tall and coming off an incredible collegiate career before touring the world with the Harlem Globetrotters.

Bill Russell at 6'10" had already led the Celtics to a championship in 1957, prior to Wilt's rookie season in 1959. By 1960, the Russell/Chamberlain rivalry had already become one of the most anticipated and iconic rivalries in sports history, a head-to-head competition that brought a flood of press coverage and endless debates while packing the arenas in both Philadelphia and Boston.

Both were physically and mentally strong, and both had incredible drive and determination to win. Wilt was an unsurpassed offensive force while Russell was a defensive genius, plus they both excelled in rebounding. They came into the league with plenty of advance notoriety from their college heroics.

Chamberlain led Kansas University to a 42–8 record and averaged nearly 30 points per game. Russell, meanwhile, averaged
20.7 points and twenty rebounds per game while leading the
University of San Francisco to a fifty-five-game winning streak
and two NCAA championships. He also starred in track and
field and became a gold medalist at the 1956 Olympics. In
Chamberlain's fourteen-year NBA career, he averaged over 30
points per game, second all-time only to Michael Jordan, while
scoring an unimaginable 100 points in a single game in 1962, a
feat that may never be equaled.

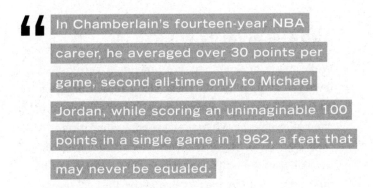

In Chamberlain's fourteen-year NBA career, he averaged over 30 points per game, second all-time only to Michael Jordan, while scoring an unimaginable 100 points in a single game in 1962, a feat that may never be equaled.

He also enjoyed a season in which he averaged 50.4 points
per game, something no one has ever come remotely close to
accomplishing. Chamberlain led the league in rebounding
eleven times and holds the single game record at fifty-five
against, of all teams, the Boston Celtics.

During Russell's thirteen-year career he averaged over twenty
rebounds for ten straight seasons, leading the league four times.
He led the Celtics to eleven world titles in thirteen years. This
included winning championships in two of his three years as a
player coach, while compiling a 162–84 coaching record with

coaching the Celtics. In head to head Celtics-Warriors match-ups, Russell's Celtics won the battle 87 to 60.

The rivalry was a major boost for the league. The NBA ben-efitted from consistent sellout crowds for their matchups, and strong ratings once television deals were in place. It was a ri-valry that also boosted attendance across the league as fans turned out to see one of the two larger-than-life superstars in action when they came to their local arena. There were also numerous articles written by leading sportswriters about the two big men, either together or individually, making them household sports names, while marketing the NBA.

▪ AND THE RIVALRY WINNER IS:

While many of Chamberlain's individual accomplish-ments certainly surpassed those of Bill Russell, or almost anyone to ever play the game, the 11–2 lead by Russell, in championships, gave him the clear edge when it came to team leadership. Perhaps Chamberlain's amazing individ-ual skills and Russell's team leadership abilities can be best summed up by the fact that in the 1961–62 season, when Chamberlain averaged 50 points per game, Russell won the MVP. And yet, the debate continues even today.

Marketing to a New Coast

Often a business is spurred to make a transition, based on the success of transitions in other businesses, or industries. This was largely the case for the NBA heading to the West Coast. It was during the Podoloff era that the league expanded geographi-cally, much the way major league baseball had done in 1957 when the Dodgers and Giants moved from New York to Los Angeles and San Francisco respectively. It was not by coincidence that the owner of the Minnesota Lakers, Bob Short, decided to head west after watching the success of two prominent baseball franchises. There was also a lull in the success for the Minneapolis Lakers after the retirement of George Mikan. In fact, the team was struggling both on the court and off, losing games and money. As a result, in 1960 the NBA saw the Minneapolis Lakers, one of the league's premiere franchises, move to Los Angeles.

Another reason for the move was that major league baseball was also moving the Washington Senators franchise to Minneapolis, which was thought would create too much competition for the Lakers. At first the team owners voted against the move, but at the time, a brand-new competitive league, the American Basketball League (ABL) was also planning to have a team in the City of Angels. The NBA team owners knew they had to compete and beat the new league to L.A. Therefore, they allowed the move, setting up one of the most iconic franchises in sports history, the Los Angeles Lakers.

The ABL, despite being formed in part by Abe Saperstein, former owner of the Globetrotters, and with a team owner by the name of George Steinbrenner, folded after two rather nondescript seasons.

The idea of heading west, however, still had appeal, and a couple of years after the Lakers' made their big move, the Philadelphia Warriors also took off for the West Coast. After being purchased by a San Francisco businessman, the Warriors packed up and moved to northern California where they settled in San Francisco. Both West Coast moves stretched the reach of the league across the country and opened the potential of drawing millions of new fans in the rapidly growing new West Coast sports market.

New Strides in the Players' Union

In 1963, Maurice Podoloff decided it was time to step down after seventeen years at the helm of the NBA. J. Walter Kennedy would step in as the league's second president shortly thereafter, taking over some significant unsettled issues. The need for a pension plan would head that list of issues and would continue as an ongoing point of contention between owners and players, with the league caught in the middle. Finally, everything came to a head at the 1964 All-Star game in Boston. The game was important to everyone concerned; it provided national television exposure for the league, and presented a unique opportunity for players to generate attention for themselves as well as the teams they represented. The players, however, used the occasion to their advantage, insinuating that they would not come out and take the court until some agreement was made regarding a pension plan. Both sides obviously had a lot to lose if the All-Star game did not take place. That afternoon, there were several conversations taking place between owners and player representatives, while the crowd took their seats in anticipation of the annual mid-season match up of the league's best talent.

Finally, minutes before game time, the new NBA commissioner J. Walter Kennedy gave his personal guarantee that adoption of a pension plan would occur at the next owners meeting. The players decided that they would take his word for it, and took the court to the delight of the fans and relief of the owners, the league, and ABC television.

When the next owners meeting took place, the owners finally established a players' pension plan through collective bargaining.

The J. Walter Kennedy Era

When J. Walter Kennedy took over as president of the NBA, there were nine teams and league attendance at roughly two million people, compared to baseball with twenty teams and attendance of over 20 million fans. There were few televised games, and as of the 1963–64 season, no team in Chicago, the third largest city at the time, after the Chicago Zephyrs moved to Baltimore. The product, however, was superb, with the likes of Jerry West, Elgin Baylor, Oscar Robertson, and other sensational athletes, along with Russell and Chamberlain. Kennedy, who had been in public relations, was confident he could grow the league, in size, attendance, and prominence while still well aware that baseball would reign supreme.

Kennedy was also quite familiar with basketball, having coached high school teams in the 1930s, working as public relations director for Notre Dame, at the BAA in the 1940s, and as publicity director for the Harlem Globetrotters in the 1950s. Then, after a slight detour into politics in the late '50s, when he became the mayor of his hometown of Stamford, Connecticut, he was elected as the new president of the NBA. His title would be changed to commissioner in 1967. Two of the most significant achievements during the Kennedy era would be expansion and television deals, which went hand in hand.

Expansion in baseball was generating a lot of excitement and TV deals were helping the teams generate revenue. The NBA owners had continued to keep tabs on the success of the large market expansion teams in baseball, which in 1962 included the Los Angeles Angels and the New York Mets.

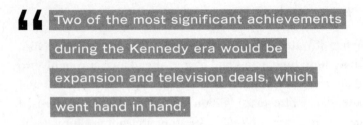

Two of the most significant achievements during the Kennedy era would be expansion and television deals, which went hand in hand.

Expansion

Expanding any business always has a list of pros and cons—with valid arguments on both sides. For one thing, it's important not to have a new location impinge upon a current one. Since the NBA in the early 1960s had only nine teams, this was unlikely to be a concern. Another issue was diluting the product, since weaker teams don't draw attention. Nonetheless, the league needed to grow and find more lucrative markets.

Expanding the NBA is also a bit tricky, since the owners have to vote on whether a new franchise should enter the league. The entrance fees for expansion teams joining the league are divided up amongst the current franchise owners, meaning that each franchise benefits financially from expansion. Of course, more teams entering the league means more ways in which to divide up league revenue. However, unlike most businesses, television would play a major role in the league's expansion. While TV ratings don't factor into the opening of a fast food franchise or even adding new branches in banking, a professional sports league can generate significant revenue from TV deals, and more teams can mean larger deals. The flip side, at the start of the 1960s, was the concern that if people could watch more games on TV they might not buy tickets. As is often the case, it would all come down to the product. If the product was top-notch entertainment, people would still want to be in the seats, regardless of TV coverage.

The first expansion team to join the league in the 1960s was a major market team, the Chicago Bulls, who joined the league in 1966 for a franchise fee of $1.6 million. The Bulls were the third NBA franchise in Chicago, after the Stags who played briefly in the 1940s, and the Packers, who are now the Washington Wizards.

It wasn't easy bringing the Bulls into the league. Dick Klein's story is recapped in Chicago Bulls history, as he was the founder and original owner of the team, spurred on by his quest to bring basketball back to the Windy City. After playing ball at Northwestern University, Klein played for the Chicago American Gears in the NBL before becoming a businessman. When he proposed bringing the Bulls into the league, he was voted down by the team owners. While Klein still had the support of league president Kennedy, who thought a team in Chicago would be an asset to the NBA, it was when Roone Arledge of ABC television also jumped on the bandwagon, (agreeing that adding Chicago to the league was, in his opinion, a great idea), that the Bulls were voted in.

The 1966–67 Bulls would become the only expansion team to make the playoffs led by Bob Boozer and veteran assist leader Guy Rodgers, who had twenty assists passing off to Wilt Chamberlain in his 100-point game for the Warriors eight years earlier. The original Bulls expansion team roster also included Jerry Sloan who would go on to be one of the team's most successful coaches.

After the Bulls broke the ice, teams rapidly began emerging over the next four years. With the huge West Coast success of the two (relocated) California teams, the Warriors and Lakers, the San Diego Rockets (now in Houston) and the Seattle Supersonics (now the Oklahoma City Thunder) joined the league in 1967. They were followed by the Milwaukee Bucks and the Phoenix Suns in 1968, and the Cleveland Cavaliers, Portland Trailblazers, the Buffalo Braves (now the L.A. Clippers), in 1970. The New Orleans Jazz, (now in Utah) would be the last team to join during Kennedy's tenure in 1974, bringing the league up to a high of eighteen teams, one more than the NBA began with prior to the contraction that marked the late 1950s. Unlike the $1.6 million Klein spent as a franchises fee for the Chicago Bulls, the Jazz owners paid $6.15 million to enter the league.

It might be noted that the 1960s was a boon for expansion across the sports world—the four major sports (baseball, football, basketball, and hockey). As William Johnson pointed in his December 1969 *Sports Illustrated* article, the four major sports went from forty-two franchises in 1959 to eighty-seven franchises in 1969, with leagues like the NHL and the NBA doubling in size.[2]

Television Deals

The NBA first signed a network television deal with DuMont prior to the 1953–54 season, a $39,000 deal to broadcast thirteen games (which were blacked out in the home team's cities). That led to a deal with NBC that brought them into the early 1960s. ABC then stepped in and broadcast games until the early 1970s. The deals continued to grow in the number of games being broadcast, and the league revenue. By the time J. Walter Kennedy stepped down as commissioner in 1975, the league had entered into a $27 million three-year deal with CBS in 1973.

While television changed the face of sports in the 1960s and the professional leagues benefitted from it, as did the players, there were concerns that television was having too big an impact on the actual sports. In basketball, for example, along with team time outs, the networks now included specific television time-outs at certain points in the game to accommodate the increased sponsorship. In a 1967 *Newsweek* article by Dick Johnson called "Breaks in the Game," Johnson pointed out Bill Russell, player-coach of the Celtics refusing to call a designated TV time-out as to not break the team's momentum during a Celtic's rally versus the 76ers. Russell was fined $50.[3] Other sports writers also voiced their disapproval, concerned that television's impact could jeopardize the sanctity of the game. But while commercials were irritating to the fans, they brought in the revenue to televise more games in an era before cable TV. And while the NBA team owners recognized the inconvenience, it was a small price to pay for the increased revenues. The players, whose salaries also benefitted from the added TV revenue, were also not too concerned.

Kareem Abdul-Jabbar and the First Sneaker Endorsement

Today, the NBA benefits from the incredible exposure and revenue earned from endorsement deals, especially when it comes to sneakers, with many players having their own brands. One of the most celebrated endorsements in sports came in 1971 when Adidas released the first player-endorsed basketball sneaker, which opened the doors to NBA superstar multimillion-dollar collaborations with sneaker companies.

The first such star to land a sneaker deal was Kareem Abdul-Jabbar, who had just changed his name from Lew Alcindor shortly after leading the Milwaukee Bucks to the NBA championship, in their second season at the end of the 1970–71 campaign. Jabbar had already risen to great notoriety prior to being the number one NBA draft pick in 1969. His college career included leading UCLA to three consecutive NCAA titles. Unlike the era of Chamberlain and Russell, television had already made a major impact by the start of the 1970s with more games being televised to a larger market, thanks to expansion.

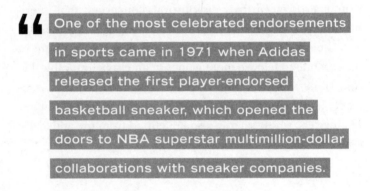

One of the most celebrated endorsements in sports came in 1971 when Adidas released the first player-endorsed basketball sneaker, which opened the doors to NBA superstar multimillion-dollar collaborations with sneaker companies.

One such nationally televised game was a legendary college meetup between the UCLA Bruins and the Houston Cougars led by future NBA hall-of famer Elvin Hayes. It was the collegiate version of the Russell-Chamberlain rivalry, billed "The Game of the Century" and played at the Astrodome in front of 52,000 fans. Houston won the game, ending UCLA's forty-seven-game winning streak. UCLA would, however, get revenge, and a title, by winning the national championship game later that season over Houston. It also introduced two future Basketball Hall of Famers to a national audience, illustrating the power of television to sell the NBA even when that was not necessarily the intent.

With his patented sky hook and charismatic smile, Jabbar came into the league, won rookie of the years and became the face of the NBA and the face of Adidas when he was approached by the sneaker giant and offered his own signature sneakers. Adidas had decided a year earlier to add to the success of their Supergrip sneaker by introducing the Superstar sneaker. With that in mind, they needed a superstar to promote the product and Jabbar had become one of the biggest names in sports. Jabbar was given $25,000 a year to endorse the sneaker, which quickly became the one of the hottest sneakers of the 1970s.

Jabbar's endorsement deal with Adidas opened the door for a marriage between professional basketball stars and signature sneakers. Later, we will talk about the most significant sneaker deals in sports, which would belong to some of the premiere NBA superstars.

Jabbar would go on to be a major force in the NBA for two decades, playing in a record nineteen All-Star games on route to becoming the league's all-time leading scorer, winning six Most Valuable Player awards, and winning the championship six times, once in Milwaukee and five times with the Lakers before being elected into the NBA Hall of Fame. Elvin Hayes went on to have a Hall of Fame career after a sixteen-year career that included a scoring title as a rookie and twelve All-Star game appearances.

Meanwhile, by the time J. Walter Kennedy retired as league commissioner in 1975, he had played a key role in changing and growing the NBA in a major way. The league had doubled in the number of teams, signed a multimillion-dollar TV deal, saw league attendance triple, and a 200 percent boost in revenue. The only thorn in Kennedy's side, and that of the league, was a rival league that came into being in the mid-1960s and outlasted Kennedy's tenure as NBA commissioner.

"Everybody pulls for David, nobody roots for Goliath."

—WILT CHAMBERLAIN

CHAPTER THREE

MAJOR COMPETITION

The Story of the ABA

There is nothing like a competitive new business to upset the status quo, and that was what happened to the NBA in the mid-1960s. For the first time, the NBA was faced with significant, direct competition. Three entrepreneurs, Dennis Arthur Murphy, who had failed to land an AFL franchise and would later become a cofounder of the World Hockey Association, joined with high caliber attorney Richard P. Tinkham, and advertising agency mogul Joe Newman to form the American Basketball Association (ABA).

It was not totally by coincidence that the ABA came into being around the time that the NFL and AFL merged. Many sportswriters and analysts believed that the goal from the start was to merge the NBA and the ABA, or at least move some teams into the NBA at some point, since joining the NBA as an expansion was far more costly.

While the NBA had managed to generate a large fan base and keep pace with the popularity of college basketball, this was a professional basketball league seeking talented athletes, some from the college ranks who were fair game, and others from NBA teams, such as Rick Barry and Billy Cunningham. In fact, as ABA cofounder Joe Newman explains it, "from the beginning, the ABA set its eyes on pulling at least enough major NBA talents to add one well-known player to each team. They made calculated choices as to who they were going after."[1]

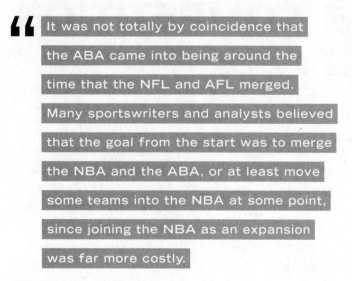

> It was not totally by coincidence that the ABA came into being around the time that the NFL and AFL merged. Many sportswriters and analysts believed that the goal from the start was to merge the NBA and the ABA, or at least move some teams into the NBA at some point, since joining the NBA as an expansion was far more costly.

Newman also explains how it all began, "Dick Tinkham, a good friend of mine, had a law firm one floor below my advertising agency in Indianapolis. While I had my share of significant clients from major movie studios to sports, Dick had some high net worth clients, plus he knew other attorneys who also had clients with deep pockets that might be interested in owning a team. Together with Dennis Arthur Murphy, Tinkham set up a meeting with a group of these wealthy individuals to discuss possible interest in owning teams in a new professional basketball league. These were not basketball people but businesspeople like trucking magnate Arthur J. Brown and show business folks like Pat Boone and Gene Autry. Along with Tinkham, who would be part of an investment group that would later own the Indiana Pacers, several agreed to put up the money, which at the time was a $30,000 franchise fee. They then created a business model, which wasn't really very good, and created an eleven-team league that started play in the fall of 1967."[2]

The original eleven franchises were in two divisions, with teams in cities that (at that time) had no NBA presence. The eastern division consisted of the Pittsburgh Pipers, Minnesota Muskies, Indiana Pacers, Kentucky Colonels, and the New Jersey Americans. The west had the New Orleans Buccaneers, Dallas Chaparrals, Denver Rockets, Houston Mavericks, Anaheim Amigos, and Oakland Oaks. Of course, Anaheim, New Jersey, and Oakland were close in proximity to NBA franchises in Los Angeles, New York, and San Francisco, and all would try to tap into those major markets even if it meant fans had to travel a little further to see their game.

Setting the League Apart

The new league was designed to be flashier, with a red, white, and blue ball, flying dunks, and on-court dance teams during time-outs and at halftime. There were also numerous promotions and gimmicks designed to excite fans and keep them coming back. The pace of play was also faster, despite a 30-second shot clock. While most of the basic rules of play were quite similar to those of the NBA, the new league introduced the three-point shot which has revolutionized the sport to this day.

The problem for the ABA was that it was going to be an uphill battle if they were going to compete with the established
NBA. "There was no national ABA TV deal, only local television," explains Newman, adding that, "you can't make it without television and sponsorship. We had local TV, but local and
national TV were like night and day."

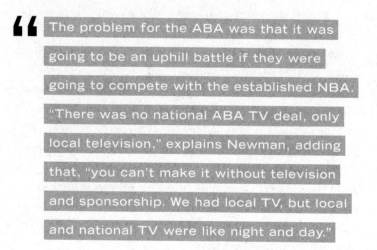

The problem for the ABA was that it was going to be an uphill battle if they were going to compete with the established NBA. "There was no national ABA TV deal, only local television," explains Newman, adding that, "you can't make it without television and sponsorship. We had local TV, but local and national TV were like night and day."

"Local TV only covered your expenses but could not support
a team, especially when it came to things like travel expenses,"
said Newman, noting that "There is only so much money you
can make from just selling tickets."[3]

Nonetheless, top talent could be found in the ABA. Star
players now had a choice of where to play, and franchises would
get into inter-league bidding wars over top talent, while some
young players would be swept into the ABA quickly, as collegiate underclassman made their way into the league, including
Spencer Hayward as a "hardship" case and Moses Malone, who

had not even gone to college—he was drafted right out of high school. This was not permitted, at that time, in the NBA.

As if creating a new league and grabbing young players before they were eligible for the NBA draft wasn't enough to cause concern, the ABA made a statement by hiring George Mikan, the NBA's original superstar, to be the first league president. At the time, Mikan was still living in Minneapolis where he ran a travel business, so the league headquarters were set up in Minneapolis.

The Competing League Sure Had Talent

The last thing a successful business wants to know is that the competition has products that will entice your customers. While the ABA franchises did not have the depth of NBA teams, they had a crowd-pleasing style of play and some excellent talent.

Through their own ABA college draft, to former NBA stars, to the Amateur Athletic Union players, and NBA rejects in search of a second chance, the ABA stocked rosters with players who simply wanted to show off their talents. And some were quite good—certainly good enough to cause NBA owners to mutter about what to do with the young upstart league.

Among the ABA's best was former NBA star Rick Barry, who left the San Francisco Warriors to spend four seasons in the ABA on three teams including the New York Nets, while posting an ABA career record 30.5 scoring average, before legal entanglements sent him back to the NBA. Then there was Dan Issel who entered the ABA in 1970, won rookie of the year, and led the Kentucky Colonels to a championship before moving with the Denver Nuggets to the NBA where he continued a long Hall-of-Fame career.

One of the most notable big men in the ABA was 7'2" Artis Gilmore, who teamed with Issel for the 1975 ABA title and later finished a stellar career with the Chicago Bulls in the NBA. The "Ice Man" George Gervin was a natural-born shooter who was signed by a Virginia Squires scout while initially playing for the Pontiac (Michigan) Chaparrals of the Continental Basketball Association. He started his ABA career in 1972. Within a year he emerged as a young star and after being traded to San Antonio, he would enjoy an illustrious career that later saw him shift from the ABA to the NBA with the Spurs, where he would win four scoring titles. Meanwhile, Louie Dampier was one of the faces always associated with the ABA. He was the original king of the three-point shot, making nearly 800 three-point field goals in his ABA career that spanned all nine years of the league's existence.

Then there was Julius Erving, Dr. J, one of basketball's legendary players, who began his Hall-of-Fame career in the ABA, winning two scoring titles for Virginia before leading the New York Nets to two ABA championships in three years. Averaging over 28 points per game in his five-year ABA career, he was one of the most exciting, dynamic players ever to step on the court, flying almost effortlessly from the foul line to slam dunk a basketball as no one had ever seen before. Erving won the first ever slam dunk contest, initiated in the ABA in 1976, and went on to play for eleven years for the Philadelphia 76ers in the NBA, leading them to a title in the 1982–83 season. Erving established himself as the face of the ABA, not through endorsements but simply by his unprecedented style of play. Dr. J would also become a significant reason why the NBA-ABA merger became a reality.

Other stars to pass through the ABA on route to NBA success were Connie Hawkins, Spencer Haywood, Moses Malone, and David Thompson, while 76ers star Billy Cunningham jumped to the ABA and then back to the 76ers where he would finish his playing career and then become a head coach, leading the 76ers to a championship in the 1982–83 season.

Of course, not all of these moves from one league to the other went smoothly. In fact, the courts, and not just the basketball courts, were seeing a lot of activity in the battle for players. Yet the NBA executives never outwardly showed great concern over the ABA. Business proceeding as usual—the senior league did not try gimmicks or changing the face of their game to compete with the younger league. The overall sense was that the NBA needed only to maintain stability and provide a marketable product and the ABA would disappear. Those who had long ties with the league, such as J. Walter Kennedy, were well aware of how long it took for the NBA franchises, and the league, to become profitable, and as long as the ABA did not have the revenue from network television, there was no real reason for concern . . . and yet, owners were not happy, especially when it came to making concerted efforts to poach their players.

The Haywood Rule

One of the most significant battles involving the two professional leagues, as well as the NCAA, involved a young player named Spencer Haywood, who was signed as an underclassman by the ABA. Haywood burst onto the scene with a spectacular rookie season, averaging 30 points and 19.5 rebounds per game on route to leading the Denver Rockets to the ABA Western Division title, and winning both the league MVP and the Rookie of the Year award. Meanwhile, the NBA and the NCAA were not happy about a professional league signing an underclassman.

The ABA claimed a hardship rule which essentially meant they could sign players who were financially unable to continue college. While the NBA had no control over ABA rules, the league knew this could open a can of worms, with other players claiming hardship and leaving school to play professionally in the new league. The door opened for NBA involvement when the Denver Rockets gave Haywood an extended contract worth nearly $2 million, which was unheard of for a first-year player. Haywood would have gladly stayed in the ABA for years had he and his attorney not realized that the vast majority of the money was going to be part of an annuity, which he could not touch until he turned fifty. Waiting nearly thirty years for his money did not sit well with Haywood who was also being pursued by the Seattle Supersonics, who then signed Haywood to a six-year $1.5 million contract with no annuities attached.

Now that he was in the NBA, the league, led by J. Walter Kennedy, sued both Haywood and the owners of the Supersonics for signing him. Haywood and his attorney claimed the NBA was in violation of the Sherman Antitrust Act. In an effort to outlaw monopolistic business practices, the Sherman Antitrust Act was signed into law back in 1890.

Haywood's attorneys claimed that the NBA was acting as a monopoly because the NBA draft put a restraint on trade and was therefore acting illegally in accordance with the Sherman Act. Initially the case was filed in United States District Court for the Central District of California, which issued an injunction in Haywood's favor. The injunction stated:

> If Haywood is unable to continue to play professional basketball for Seattle, he will suffer irreparable injury in that a substantial part of his playing career will have been dissipated, his physical condition, skills, and coordination will deteriorate from lack of

high-level competition, his public acceptance as a super star will diminish to the detriment of his career, his self-esteem, and his pride will have been injured and a great injustice will be perpetrated on him.[4]

The NBA appealed to the Ninth Circuit Court of Appeals, which stayed the injunction, essentially shutting down the case temporarily. The case was then appealed all the way up to the United States Supreme Court, which ruled 7–2 in Haywood's favor in 1971. This resulted, not only in a marvelous career with the Seattle Supersonics for Haywood, but more significantly, in the NBA introducing a hardship rule for players who could prove financial hardship to enter the NBA as an underclassman, or directly out of high school. This allowed the likes of Kobe Bryant and LeBron James to forego college completely, with many other players leaving college early. In the end, the Haywood Rule, as it was known, had a huge impact upon the NBA.

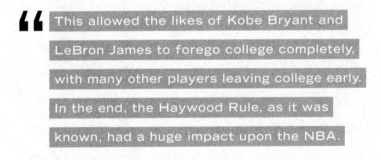

> " This allowed the likes of Kobe Bryant and LeBron James to forego college completely, with many other players leaving college early. In the end, the Haywood Rule, as it was known, had a huge impact upon the NBA.

The Merger

By 1976, after nine years, the ABA was struggling, and the inevitable finally became a reality. Many players had come and gone in the ABA, and many battles had been waged to land the best talent. Both sides won some and lost others, but the ABA was simply not making money. Some saw the league as growing, noting how it took the NBA more than a decade to gain traction. The reality, however, was that by the mid-1970s it was impossible to sustain a league without a national TV deal. *Newsweek* magazine saw the failure of the ABA to sign Lew Alcindor as a potential death knell for the league. If nothing else, the ABA was a phenomenon unto itself—a league that had some amazing talent, great spirit, and revolutionary ideas. But without a merger, or a TV deal, most people connected with either league sensed the league could only survive for so long.

The idea of a merger had come up in discussions several years earlier, after just three ABA seasons. In 1970, NBA owners voted in favor of bringing the leagues together. Owners didn't like the idea of having to pay tremendous numbers to top stars in an era before mega TV contracts meant multimillions of dollars in revenue. Oscar Robertson, then head of the NBPA, led the association in filing a lawsuit against the NBA on the grounds of antitrust in order to squelch such a merger. It took six years to settle the legal battle which made any such merger virtually impossible.

Holding Their Own

During the six years until the merger (1970–1976), the NBA remained confident that it was the superior league to the upstart ABA. But when they did put their theory to the test on the hardwood, the ABA did more than just hold their own. Prior to the 1971–72 season the ABA and NBA met in a pre-season All-Star game, which the NBA won by just five points. Over the next several years, teams from each league met in exhibition games. Between 1971 and 1975, the year prior to the merger, the teams played nearly 100 games and the ABA won more than 60 percent of them. The NBA was both humbled and excited. The senior league was expected to dominate, but were surprised at the level of talent that met them on the court. On the other hand, knowing a merger was in the cards, the NBA recognized that they would be getting some very worthy players. In fact, in the first season after the merger, ten of the twenty-four All-Stars were former ABA players.

While many teams came and went in the ABA, due to financial issues (much like those in the early years of the NBA), the remaining six teams in 1976 (when the merger became a reality) included the New York Nets, San Antonio Spurs, Indiana Pacers, Denver Nuggets, Kentucky Colonels, and the St. Louis Spirits.

Leading the merger talks for the NBA was lead attorney David Stern and for the ABA was cofounder Dick Tinkham. "None of the ABA teams were making any money and they were going to go broke if they weren't absorbed by the NBA, which had an ensuing TV deal. It [the merger] was largely driven by television," Joe Newman explained.[5]

Bob Wussler, then president of CBS, had renegotiated a new four-year television contract with the NBA that would give the league $21 million in the first two years and $22 million for the final two years. The network also offered the NBA an additional $5 million as an incentive if up to four new franchises from the ABA were accepted into the NBA.

On June 18, 1976, NBA owners, after years of talking about the possibility of a merger, voted 17–1 to merge with the ABA. The Denver Nuggets, Indiana Pacers, New York Nets, and San Antonio Spurs all joined the league. They were, however, not allowed to participate in the 1976 NBA college draft.

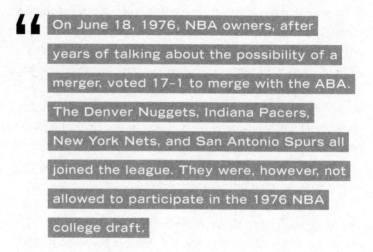

" On June 18, 1976, NBA owners, after years of talking about the possibility of a merger, voted 17–1 to merge with the ABA. The Denver Nuggets, Indiana Pacers, New York Nets, and San Antonio Spurs all joined the league. They were, however, not allowed to participate in the 1976 NBA college draft.

"Two teams didn't make it to the NBA, they didn't have the same drawing power of the others and the NBA only wanted to keep no more than four ABA teams in the merger as stipulated in the TV deal. The St. Louis Spirits didn't make the league, so the owners sued the NBA," explains Newman. "They ended up with an incredible deal which gave them revenues in perpetuity that have reached nearly half a billion dollars and will continue as long as the NBA remains in business." This deal is widely considered one of the few awful deals made by the NBA.

"The Kentucky Colonels, the other team that didn't get into the NBA, had some top players, and were owned by a group of investors led by John Y. Brown, who purchased Kentucky Fried Chicken from Colonel Sanders. He had the money to bring them into the league, but the NBA was clear, no more than four teams," says Newman.[6] The players from the Colonels and Spirits were then absorbed by NBA teams in a dispersal draft in which Kentucky center, Artis Gilmore, was the first player selected by the Chicago Bulls.

Of course, the NBA imposed certain stipulations that had to be met before the teams could enter the league. The stipulations were discussed by the owners and the league in an effort to make sure the teams entering the league would be in accordance with other league policies and financially stable. While the end result was four new NBA teams, Stern and Tinkham, along with many other attorneys working for and representing the owners' interests, all had a lot of details to contend with. For example, the New York Nets had to pay the New York Knicks $4.8 million as compensation for also being in the New York market. That was on top of the $3.2 million that each of the ABA teams would pay the NBA for entering the league. The $8 million price tag resulted in the Nets having to enter the NBA on a bleak note, selling the contract of Julius Erving to the Philadelphia 76ers right before the start of the Nets' first NBA season, then having to repay some of the money season ticket holders had paid to see Dr. J and the Nets.

Joe Newman tells his story of helping the Indiana Pacers over a hurdle to get then securely into the NBA. "The Pacers needed to meet a high number of season tickets sold to qualify for the NBA. At the time, I owned Joe Newman Advertising, and one of our many clients was the Indiana Pacers of the ABA, so I played a role in the process and actually helped save the team. Although this story was never published, I led a grassroots campaign to get out and sell tickets quickly to meet the NBA season ticket sales mandate. I hired roughly twenty-five salesmen, shoe salesmen, aluminum siding salesmen, carpet salesmen, or any other good salesmen I could find and put them in Indiana Pacers T-shirts. Then I sent them out selling Pacers' tickets. They went into every office building in the city and anywhere else they could go to sell tickets. At the time, tickets cost about $10 to $12 per game. This makeshift sales team was paid every day in cash and every time they sold forty tickets, we'd ring the bell and add to the sales total, which we kept posting in the Indianapolis newspapers. These guys sold thousands and thousands of individual tickets that we combined to turn into season tickets. They were persistent, don't take no for an answer kind of guys— it was like having Willie Loman show up on your porch selling basketball tickets. Of course, they were selling a good product— the Pacers had some great players including George McGinnis, Mel Daniels, and Roger Brown. They had won a couple of ABA titles and now you could watch them play against established NBA teams like the Lakers and Celtics. My grassroots sales plan worked, and we helped the Pacers make their way into the NBA by doing our part to fill up Market Square Arena."[7]

Gone but Not Forgotten

The impact of the ABA is still felt in the NBA today as three-point shots rain down upon the baskets at an ever-increasing rate, changing the style of play. The Slam Dunk contest, along with a three-point shooting contest are now features of the NBA All-Star weekend. The whole idea of the slam dunk, which originated as an art form in the ABA, became more prominent in the NBA. The league utilized the ingenuity that can often come with a business merger, focusing on some of the most fan appealing aspects of the ABA.

Then, of course, the Spencer Haywood rule brought youth to the league with players starting their careers earlier.

From a business standpoint, however, the battle with the ABA tested the resolve of the NBA and the franchise owners. The relationship between owners and players was strained, especially while everyone involved waited out the lawsuit filed by Oscar

Robertson which delayed a possible merger by six years. The NBA, however, as an established business dealing with a young competitor knew they had more resources at their disposal, including an established product, fan base, and more large market teams. After all, as the ABA shrunk on their accord, the NBA had more quality players than the new league could sign. Therefore, the NBA's plan, despite nearly a decade of strained relationships, worked perfectly. Monitor the competition, maintain the highest-level product and otherwise, do nothing to boost fan interest in the competition. The NBA knew a merger would happen, on their terms, it was just a matter of how and when.

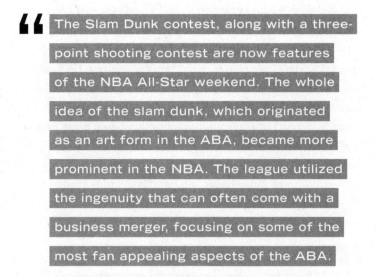

The Slam Dunk contest, along with a three-point shooting contest are now features of the NBA All-Star weekend. The whole idea of the slam dunk, which originated as an art form in the ABA, became more prominent in the NBA. The league utilized the ingenuity that can often come with a business merger, focusing on some of the most fan appealing aspects of the ABA.

"Had the ABA come along fifteen or twenty years earlier, they might have built the same momentum that the NBA had created by the time the new league came to pass," adds Newman, noting that, "the only thing the NBA passed up on was the red, white, and blue basketball."[8] It was originally a decision by a nearsighted George Mikan who once said, of the basketball, "Let's be creative and dye the damn thing red, white, and blue. That was something you could see from the balcony, you could see it on television."[9]

The ABA Revival

Much to the surprise of many people, in 2000, the ABA returned as a semiprofessional league with the "blessing" of the NBA. "It just so happened that I bumped into Dick Tinkham by chance. I hadn't seen him in well over a decade," recalls Joe Newman. "He asked what I had been up to and I told him that I had sold my advertising agency and retired in 1983. Then I bought sixteen radio stations, but I didn't like the direction radio was taking, so I sold my radio stations and I retired again in 1998. There was a pause, and he then asked me if I thought we could bring back the ABA. I told him I'd love to bring it back but not the way it was. It needed diversification, especially when it came to owning a team, which is still an issue today. You shouldn't have to be Michael Jordan, Magic Johnson, or Jay-Z to be a team owner. I also want it to be fan-friendly and affordable, plus I didn't want to get caught up in all the collective bargaining issues."[10]

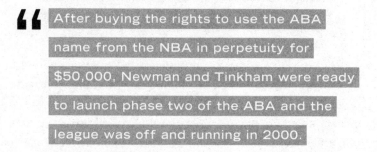

After buying the rights to use the ABA name from the NBA in perpetuity for $50,000, Newman and Tinkham were ready to launch phase two of the ABA and the league was off and running in 2000.

After buying the rights to use the ABA name from the NBA in perpetuity for $50,000, Newman and Tinkham were ready to launch phase two of the ABA and the league was off and running in 2000. Fast forward and some twenty years later, and there are nearly 150 teams all around the country in six divisions. Newman, CEO of the league, also got the diversity he was seeking. "Roughly 75 percent of the team owners are African American, Asian, Hispanic or women, and we have fabulous players in a fan-friendly, affordable league. It's a fast pace, full court brand of basketball. Our rules are a combination of the NBA, NCAA and international rules, with a few of our own rules designed to make it faster and more exciting. The business model is the best business model in professional sports, providing for everyone involved. It includes the organization, training, marketing, tickets/sponsorships, press/media relations, community relations, internships, promotions, merchandising, and the website and social media as parts of the business model that allow franchises to be successful," says Newman, who's now in his 80s, running the show and totally loving it. "I want the teams to be successful,"[11] he added. And while there have been casualties along the way, the newly revamped ABA continues to grow with new teams popping up in cities and counties all over the country each year and now offer streaming games on ABA TV on the internet. There's also an ABA Australia, ABA Mexico, and the WABA.

In essence, the ABA legacy continues!

"I've had enough
   success for two lifetimes,
   my success is talent
   put together with hard
   work and luck."

—KAREEM ABDUL-JABBAR

CHAPTER FOUR

EVOLUTION

From Tape Delay to MJ

Despite four former ABA teams entering the NBA and bringing some additional talent into the league, the late 1970s saw a slight downturn for the league. The quality of the product was still good basketball, but new league ambassadors were missing. Julius Erving, George Gervin, Kareem Abdul-Jabbar, and Pistol Pete Maravich were still All-Stars who could dazzle fans, but they had all been doing so for at least eight years by the start of the 1979–80 season. There was also a growing problem with drug use by players, which the league addressed with stricter rules. Additionally, a number of teams were struggling financially. Expansion had brought the league up to twenty-two teams, but several lacked major star power and, as a result, there were fewer marquee matchups. Surprisingly some teams in markets, such as Chicago, New York, Los Angeles, Philadelphia, and Golden State were dropping in attendance.

Competition between the NBA and the ABA drove up costs with the war for players taking salaries up to a new level. Such huge salaries were not yet widely accepted in sports and many fans didn't like that the idea of players getting massive paychecks. Television ratings were also down as NBA fans had become somewhat indifferent to the league. Even Jerry West, former star player and coach of the Lakers at the time, felt the lack of enthusiasm in a major basketball town. "People I talk to around Los Angeles all tell me that there isn't a great deal of interest in either the Lakers or the NBA," said West in a February 26, 1979, *Sports Illustrated* article.[1]

In the *Sports Illustrated* article, writer John Papanek also points to Larry O'Brien referring to the league as being stable, since teams are not losing money. The article noted, "stability can also imply stagnation, and that is precisely what those twin indicators of public appeal—attendance and television ratings—show. Both are disappointing, raising serious questions about the future of the sport. " To hammer home the point, Papanek put a concerning number that national television ratings were down a whopping 26 percent. "The first four regular-season Sunday CBS telecasts were beaten soundly by everything the other networks threw at them, including Superstars and boxing (ABC), and college basketball (NBC)," wrote Papanek.[2]

Clearly, the NBA was having trouble. Something needed to happen to jumpstart the league. But, unlike many businesses that will turn to research and development to create new products, success in the NBA depends on scouting, recruiting, drafting, and signing the brightest and best talent. This could take some time, and a little luck—you couldn't just create the next Chamberlain-Russell rivalry, or count on finding another Kareem Abdul-Jabbar. And, unlike the ABA, the NBA was not opting for promotional gimmicks to fill seats. In short, while the league could clean up internal issues, such as taking a stronger stance on drug usage and work on marketing campaigns to broaden the league's image, the NBA still needed a boost.

Great Rivalry II:
The One That Resurrected the NBA

Starting in the early days of the NBA, standout college players were the backbone behind driving the league forward. It was, to some degree, akin to the research and development found in more traditional business. Only the league had not yet discovered ways in which to develop young talent, as they do today with global basketball camps and schools so they had to rely on the college draft.

As good fortune would have it, the NBA found their future in two NCAA players that would forever change the face of basketball. They came from West Baden Springs, Indiana, and Lansing, Michigan, and ended up enshrined in Springfield, Massachusetts, in the Basketball Hall of Fame.

Ervin "Magic" Johnson and Larry Bird had established themselves as two of the biggest stars of the NCAA. By the end of the 1978–79 season, Bird had led the number one seeded Indiana State Sycamores to an unbeaten season at 33–0. Johnson, meanwhile, had orchestrated the number three seeded Michigan State Spartans to a 25–6 record. Their matchup in the NCAA Championship propelled the already national popularity of college basketball to new heights with a record-breaking Nielson television rating of 24.1, as Johnson worked his magic and led Michigan State to a 75–64 upset win over Bird and the Sycamores.

As college basketball coach and commentator Al McGuire was quoted as saying in the 2009 Seth David book, *When March*

Went Mad: The Game That Transformed Basketball: "The college game was already on the launching pad, and then Bird and Magic came along and pushed the button."[3]

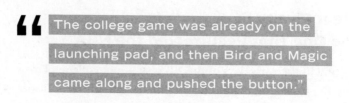

" The college game was already on the launching pad, and then Bird and Magic came along and pushed the button."

Bird and Magic were NBA rookies in the 1979–80 season and following their college title game the rivalry would become something special. Unlike Chamberlain and Russell, TV coverage by 1980 had changed significantly, so this rivalry could play out in front of millions of viewers on national television. There were also far more endorsement possibilities, so both players could quickly become the new faces to the league, and the NBA was prepared to do their fair share of marketing.

Breaking Bread

While the two superstars became legendary performers on the court, as well as household names, they also enjoyed a good friendship, which began while shooting Converse sneakers commercials in the mid-1980s that featured both stars. As the now well-documented story goes, they "broke bread together" while shooting a commercial in French Lick, Indiana, near Bird's family home. When the crew broke for lunch, Magic was heading to his trailer to grab a bite when Larry caught up to him and invited him for a home-cooked meal. Magic, glad to get off the set for a little while accepted the invitation from his commercial costar and longtime rival.

They went back to Larry's mom's house, where she made them lunch. Having been thrust into the roles of intense rivals in college, and playing for two NBA teams, each with a long-time devoted fanbase that harbored animosity toward the other team, it was difficult to set aside the perception of all those around them, that they also didn't like each other. But a big hug from Bird's mom and a home-cooked meal were the ice breakers that made Magic feel comfortable and welcome. The truth was that they had never actually sat down and had a conversation. Away from the limelight, they finally had an opportunity to converse without a swarm of media and a film crew around them. Still rivals on the court, they developed a long-time friendship.

Yet once they stepped onto the hardwood, they were both totally intensely driven to win a championship. Their individual games were different, with Bird being the better outside shooter and rebounder, while Magic was an amazing ball handler and passer, contributing to Kareem Abdul-Jabbar's all-time scoring record by hitting him as often as possible. The presence of Kareem allowed Magic to score less while quarterbacking the team with an uncanny sense of everything taking place on the court.

By the end of their careers they had each posted tremendous numbers in almost the same number of games (Magic with 906, Bird with 897). Bird averaged 24.3 points, 10 rebounds, and 6.2 assists per game, while making twelve All-Star appearances and winning three titles. Johnson averaged 19.5 points per game, 7.2 rebounds, and 11.5 assists per game, while also making twelve All-Star appearances and winning five championships. They each made the All-NBA first team ten times, and each landed in the Basketball Hall of Fame while achieving legendary status.

Yet it's more than the numbers. From a business standpoint, there were plenty of storylines to market this rivalry in both major cities, as well as across the country. Bird was a poor kid from a small town who had become a big city sports icon in Boston, a serious sports-minded town with a great love for their teams and their players. Magic was a poor urban kid, yet he was flashy, and ideal for Hollywood, and the slew of fans who loved their Lakers.

Neither Bird nor Magic ever considered being traded. Both wanted to remain with the teams that had drafted them for their entire careers—a loyalty which was already becoming a rarity in sports.

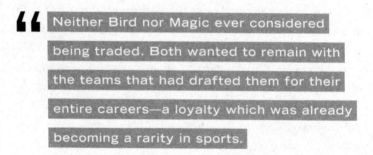

" Neither Bird nor Magic ever considered being traded. Both wanted to remain with the teams that had drafted them for their entire careers—a loyalty which was already becoming a rarity in sports.

All of these storylines helped the league market the players to the rest of the country for the remainder of the decade, with each team doing their part to surround the rivals with top talent leading to winning seasons.

By the early 1990s, Bird would begin to experience back pain and he finally called it quits after a thirteen-year career. Magic's career came to an end on November 7, 1991, when he made the shocking announcement that he had HIV. Before making the historic public statement to the media, and the world, Magic called a few people, those with whom he felt particularly close—Larry Bird was one of those few people. Johnson made it clear that he would beat this. Bird, like so many others around the game, across the NBA and around the globe, was stunned at the news but let Magic know he was rooting for him 100 percent. Within minutes after the announcement, in the pre-internet days, prayers and positive thoughts for Magic came pouring into the league office, the Lakers office, and sports media outlets from everywhere. Magic had played thirteen years in the NBA. He later made a brief return to the Lakers in 1996 and then called it quits for good. More than three decades later, Magic is still going strong, proving that he was a champion both on and off the court. He remains an iconic, legendary figure, one whose impact on the league has never dissipated.

THE MEN WHO SAVED THE NBA

In a March 2017 article for the online basketball media site fadeawayworld.com, journalist Sam Beidokhti wrote of Bird and Magic:

"They were the ones that saved the NBA. When they came into the NBA, the finals were on tape delay, the league was losing money, and it looked as though the NBA was about to fail. Yet, with Bird and Magic, the NBA got stars that could carry the league forward. It also was a great story that could be sold. They combined the substance of the '60s with the style of the '70s to create a new product that was enjoyable to watch."[4]

The Changing Impact of Television Coverage

The NBA had a long-standing relationship with television, which by the 1970s was true of all of the major professional sports leagues. NBA television ratings, however, by the mid-70s did not justify primetime broadcasting. Other than the CBS Sunday afternoon double headers, the league was seeing little broadcast time on the network. Local television carried NBA and college games, but the significant revenue came from major network exposure.

When it came time for the playoffs, CBS decided to put some games on tape delay so they would not preempt their primetime schedule. The late-night (11:30) tape-delayed era began in 1976 and continued into the early 1980s. The tape-delayed broadcasts generated even lower ratings as fan interest continued to diminish.

Television played a major role in controlling the starting times of televised games, as it does today. The difference in the mid to late '70s and the early '80s from current sports programming, was that the product was not as salable, leaving CBS to prioritize regular programming over NBA games and the league could do little about it. That would soon change.

The early 1980s saw the influx of cable TV with ESPN and the USA Network. CBS was becoming aware that there were other places to watch NBA games, so they made sure to lock up Boston Celtics or L.A. Lakers games on Sundays as often as possible. By 1982, for the first time in several years, all of the NBA finals were aired in primetime. That series pitted Magic Johnson and Kareem Abdul-Jabbar of the Lakers against the Philadelphia 76ers featuring Dr. J and Darryl Dawkins, who despite being three inches shorter than Jabbar outweighed him by 25 pounds and was known for his brute strength, shattering backboards on occasion. These were players fans wanted to watch. It was also a matchup of major market East and West Coast teams.

Television ratings continued to grow with the reemergence of the league's popularity led by the fan base for the Lakers and Celtics. The rivalry between Bird and Johnson, and their respective teams, put the NBA back on solid ground with television showcasing the product coast to coast, along with the brand ambassadors, who appeared in a host of TV commercials and on various talk shows.

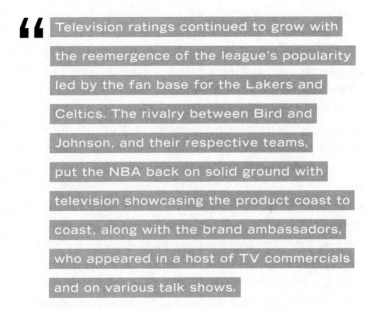

Television ratings continued to grow with the reemergence of the league's popularity led by the fan base for the Lakers and Celtics. The rivalry between Bird and Johnson, and their respective teams, put the NBA back on solid ground with television showcasing the product coast to coast, along with the brand ambassadors, who appeared in a host of TV commercials and on various talk shows.

During this time, the league was run by the third NBA commissioner Larry O'Brien. He held the job for nine years, coming from politics into the NBA. O'Brien had worked with John

Kennedy in 1959, LBJ in the mid-1960s, and served as chairman of the Democratic National Convention in Miami in 1972. He also happened to have an office in a Washington hotel known as Watergate, which was targeted in the famous break-in.

After serving in politics and playing a role in the Watergate scandal, the NBA certainly seemed like a far less contentious job. While the NBA-ABA merger, and subsequent TV deal with CBS had been brewing for some time, O'Brien was at the helm when they were signed. He held onto the league through the rocky 1970s and was there when the Bird/Magic rivalry jolted the league back on the right track.

Despite the lull in league interest in the 1970s, O'Brien had made an impact. He established an NBA scholarship program, put together an anti-drug program, and was on board during the discussions regarding a salary cap in 1983 that would put a lid, of sorts, on out-of-control salaries. Then, in 1983, O'Brien handed the reigns over to David Stern, who had a less dramatic background than O'Brien's political career. He did, however, have nearly two decades of experience working with the NBA.

Stern knew how things were done in the league from top to bottom having worked as an outside counsel for the league since 1966 and on the NBA staff as the league's executive council since 1978. He worked closely with J. Walter Kennedy and Larry O'Brien on many key negotiations including the NBA-ABA merger. Stern was always looking out for the league's best interest and, as a result, the owners knew they didn't have to look outside the organization when they had a strong person to promote from within. He became the fourth commissioner of the NBA.

The Ultimate Matchup

Shortly after stepping into the role of commissioner, Stern was greeted by some of the most significant players ever to enter the league, including Michael Jordan, Charles Barkley, and Hakeem Olajuwon. Then, at the end of his first season as commissioner, the Celtics and Lakers renewed the classic Bird/Magic rivalry on the largest basketball stage of all—the NBA Finals. The Lakers and Celtics had battled many times in the late 1950s and early '60s, with the Celtics having the decided 7–0 edge when it came to winning championships.

Bird and a legion of sports fans had not forgotten the classic NCAA finals when Magic and Michigan State defeated Bird and Indiana State for the college title. They were ready for justice to be served. The Lakers also had a lot of support as a team that had lost to the Celtics in every one of their final's matchups. They came in as the Hollywood team with finesse and swagger up against what was considered the working man's team out of Boston. There was more than enough talent to go around besides Bird and Magic, including Kareem Abdul-Jabbar, James Worthy, and Michael Cooper on the Lakers, and Kevin McHale, Robert Parrish, and Dennis Johnson on the Celtics. There were also notable coaches Pat Riley for the Lakers, and K.C. Jones for the Celtics, both of whom would end up enshrined in the Basketball Hall of Fame.

The series went a grueling seven games, with Bird and the Celtics making it 8–0 in NBA Finals matchups with the Lakers. Not only had the series lived up to the hype and anticipation, but it provided an increase in NBA fan interest, with casual fans jumping onboard for a series featuring household names.

The Nielson Ratings were strong at 12.1 with 26 million viewers. Meanwhile, Larry Bird finally had his revenge. The teams would meet two more times in the next three years, with the Lakers winning both and ending the Celtic domination.

By the third meeting of the Lakers and Celtics in 1987, the finals set a new record with ratings of nearly 16 points (or 16 percent of households in the United States). The NBA had benefited from TV coverage for years, but it wasn't until the late 1980s that the league's ratings had reached the point that games became must-see television, and the NBA and CBS could now work together on even ground to make national games a staple of sports broadcasting and never return to the infamous "tape-delay era," as it was called.

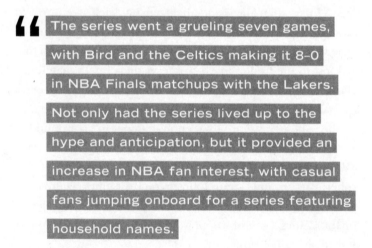

The series went a grueling seven games, with Bird and the Celtics making it 8–0 in NBA Finals matchups with the Lakers. Not only had the series lived up to the hype and anticipation, but it provided an increase in NBA fan interest, with casual fans jumping onboard for a series featuring household names.

Even after the heyday of Bird and Magic, the Celtics and Lakers would continue to be long-distance rivals for years to come. Today, with the emergence and growth of sports talk radio over the past twenty-five years, along with numerous websites, sports rivalries (real or fabricated) have taken on a new level enthusiasm. Ongoing debates and comparison of NBA teams and players continue today across the media from ESPN to Twitter collectively serving as no-cost 'round the clock promotion for the league.

One of the values of sports, as a business, is that the product is constantly being discussed and someone is always writing about it. The question is how favorably they are reporting on the business. The NBA went from a more negative portrayal in the 1970s to a positive buzz that has continued ever since once David Stern took office. This was not just good fortune, it took an ongoing effort to put league representatives (players), in front of fans as much as possible, both on and off the court, in games or involved in community activities.

David Stern Makes His Mark

While the league was on an upswing, Stern took the opportunity to expand revenue sources by expanding the league in all directions—marketing, merchandising, and licensing. "Stern and his colleagues had terrific vision," said Stephen A. Greyser, a professor of consumer marketing at the Harvard Business School. The NBA, he told journalist Glenn Rifkin, became focused on brand equity in the early 1980s, before the other sports leagues and most companies even understood the importance of the concept.[5]

To build the marketing and merchandising efforts, Stern increased the small NBA staff to over 600 people who were the beneficiaries of his infectious enthusiasm and desire to grow the brand into something huge, beyond what other leagues had done before. Doing this meant forging strategic alliances with retailers and reestablishing and building strong alliances with television. It also meant supporting brand ambassadors whose individual deals provide league visibility. As Rifkin wrote, "In its symbiotic relationships with the networks and with corporate sponsors like Nike, the NBA has garnered endless advertising and marketing goodwill without spending any of its own money."[6]

Stern also helped promote the league off the court with community outreach and involvement. He was also the first to expand upon whatever the league was currently offering. For example, the All-Star game went from a one-night East-West matchup to a three-day event, All-Star Weekend, including the slam dunk, three point and skills competitions, the rising talent game, and a celebration throughout the host city. In doing things of this nature, Stern built upon the fun and excitement of the game itself and created a bond with the fans that extended behind the court.

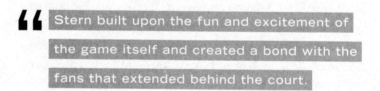

Stern built upon the fun and excitement of the game itself and created a bond with the fans that extended behind the court.

Stern attributed much of the impact he (and those working for the NBA), had upon the league, to acquiring knowledge. In a 2017 video interview on the *Forbes SportsMoney* program, he talked about his thirst for knowledge in order to do things better, and how this became the culture of the NBA. He wanted the NBA to be a learning organization and credited Adam Silver as sustaining a learning culture. He used the example of just finishing an All-Star game and afterward asking, "What did we learn? What can we learn from other events? And how can we do it better and differently next year?"

Learning not only came from what the league was doing or even what other sports leagues were doing, but from looking closely at what the most successful businesses were doing. What are the best in class doing? The idea was to see how other businesses, in other industries, handled marketing, events, globalization and so forth and to generate ideas based on this knowledge that translated to the NBA. At one point in the *Forbes* interview, Stern mentioned that he has taken time to help startups, and was often met with the question, "What does he know about startups?" Stern replied that in 1978 he was only the twenty-fourth employee hired by the NBA, meaning that it was still, in many ways a startup business. Today, the league, including the NBA, WNBA and G League, has over 3,000 employees worldwide.[7]

As is the case in most businesses, everything starts at the top, so Stern had to introduce many new ideas to owners who, like a board of directors, had to mull over those ideas and make decisions based on Stern's recommendations. Also, as is the case in business, unions often have a say in final decisions. One of the most challenging roles of each NBA commissioner has always been navigating the relationship between the owners and the NBA Players Association (NBPA). Stern's approach, bringing in more revenue through marketing, merchandising, and sponsorships, took everything up to a higher level. More money in league revenue meant that all teams rise. He also instituted a salary cap of $3.6 million in an effort to balance the league, giving the small market teams a better opportunity to sign star players and remain competitive. This worked, as evidenced by the amazing success of the San Antonio Spurs.

■ FREE AGENCY:
AN UNOBTRUSIVE INTRODUCTION

When you consider the instantaneous round-the-globe news and boundless analysis that NBA free agent signings generate today, it's almost unimaginable how quietly unrestricted free agency emerged in the league. It was in 1988, during David Stern's tenure as NBA commissioner, that a 6'10" All-Star forward, Tom Chambers, who averaged over 20 points a game for the Seattle Supersonics, signed a free agency deal to play for the Phoenix Suns. The signing did not generate much attention at the time, but it was historic; it was first signing of an unrestricted free agent in the NBA. Part of the Collective Bargaining Agreement (CBA) between the league and the players union allowed for players to become unrestricted free agents if they met certain criteria. They had to have completed two NBA contracts and been in the league at least seven years. Chambers fit both categories and signed the new contract shortly after finding out that the latest CBA was ratified.

Limited *free agency* through the elimination of "option" clauses that bound players to teams in perpetuity had existed since 1976, but they were not the same as unrestricted free agency. While there was speculation on what this could mean for player movement, few people realized how immense the impact would be on the league.

Since the NBA is about the individual franchises that make up the league, Stern continued to work on increasing the owners' take, which would stabilize the teams that were struggling.

When Stern initially took office, the twenty-three NBA teams were collectively worth $400 million, when he left office, they were worth nearly that much individually. New teams entered the league for a $6 million expansion fee. That rose to over $300 million by the time Stern left. Yet, despite rising franchise fees, owners still wanted to be a part of the league, and this led to more expansion.

In 1988, two teams joined the league, and in 1989, two more followed. They were the first expansion teams since the 1980 addition of the Dallas Mavericks. The Miami Heat and Orlando Magic brought teams to Florida for the first time, and since joining the league, the Heat have won three NBA titles. The other two teams were the Charlotte Hornets and the Minnesota Timberwolves. While the city of Charlotte was brand-new to the league, Minnesota was gaining a franchise for the first time in nearly three decades. While expansion teams typically struggle, it had become easier for them to start making some headway thanks to free agency. And thanks to TV deals, merchandising, and sponsorship, it became easier for new teams to manage financially than it was for teams playing in the early years of the league that had to survive primarily on ticket sales.

The MJ Era

As athletes got faster afoot, quicker, stronger, and more durable over the years, such athletic prowess continued to be on display in the NBA. From Russell and Chamberlain to Oscar Robertson, Julius Irving, and Magic Johnson, the bar kept rising when it came to outperforming the best of the best in NBA history. The league was very fortunate that the product, professional basketball, just kept getting better.

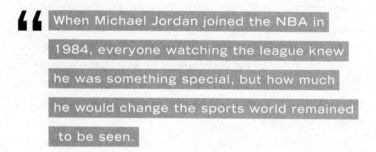

When Michael Jordan joined the NBA in 1984, everyone watching the league knew he was something special, but how much he would change the sports world remained to be seen.

When Michael Jordan joined the NBA in 1984, everyone watching the league knew he was something special, but how much he would change the sports world remained to be seen. In a thirteen-year career, interrupted twice by retirement, Jordan dazzled fans worldwide, leading the Chicago Bulls to their first ever NBA title, and five more to follow. Had Michael not left basketball to play baseball for two seasons (to honor his slain father, who had always wanted him to be a baseball player), it's very possible that the Bulls would have won eight titles in a row rather than a very impressive six over eight years. Jordan broke records, becoming the first player to lead the league in scoring for ten consecutive seasons, and winning five MVP awards. Then there were the earnings from the many endorsements off-the court. According to *Forbes*, Michael Jordan is still earning $60 million annually off his shoe sales. It was his Air Jordans that launched the culture of specially designed basketball shoes. They would quickly become the greatest selling sports shoes in history. When film director Spike Lee directed Jordan's Nike commercials using the slogan, "It's gotta be the shoes" with the logo of Jordan flying through the air, as he did while winning the league's first two slam dunk contests, it defined the Jordan era. He also signed deals with Gatorade, Upper Deck, Hanes, Coca-Cola, McDonald's, Chevrolet, General Mills, and many other brands. Yet, the shoes are a reason why Jordan still makes more money today than any other NBA athlete.

Jordan brought in NBA revenue like nobody had previously before. Estimates for the 1999–2000 season, after Jordan's retirement from the Bulls, was that the league could lose more than 10 percent of its revenue, which at the time was $2 billion. *Forbes* estimated, just prior to his last NBA Finals appearance that Michael had a $10 billion impact on the economy, from filling seats to a boost in TV revenues plus the millions of items sold around the world.

Jordan's successful film debut, starring with a host of Looney Tunes characters and a few other NBAers in *Space Jam* put the NBA in front of many young fans, while seeing Will Smith wearing Jordans in his TV series *The Fresh Prince of Bel-Air*, or hip-hop stars, such as Nas, Drake, and DJ Khaled donning the shoes in videos helped establish another growing market.

Jordan is still considered by most fans of the league to be the greatest to ever play the game and he became an iconic figure that forever changed the NBA.

"Be positive and work hard. I think it's possible to overcome anything, if you're willing to work at it."

—SHERYL SWOOPES

CHAPTER FIVE

THE WNBA

I t all began during the David Stern era, when the concept of a professional basketball league for women was launched in conjunction with the NBA. The initial battle cry, "We've Got Next," was first declared at an NBA board meeting and the WNBA was founded shortly thereafter. The idea was largely to diversify and reach out to a new market, women athletes and their fans, many of which had cheered their college teams on to victory. It was also a manner in which to further introduce the game to girls.

The affiliation with the NBA allowed the new league to cut many corners, such as easing the search for venues and support staff. Most of the rules were similar to those of the NBA, with some influence from the NCAA: for example, the WNBA began by playing two 20-minute halves instead of four 12-minute quarters (the WNBA now plays four 10-minute quarters). The ball was slightly smaller and the three-point line a little closer, but the basic rules and the league structure were very similar to the NBA.

The eight original teams, all in NBA cities, were the Charlotte Sting, Cleveland Rockets, Houston Comets, Los Angeles Sparks, New York Liberty, Phoenix Mercury, Sacramento Monarchs, and the Utah Starzz. The teams were owned by the NBA team owners and governed in the same manner. The season, however, would be considerably shorter than the eighty-two game NBA season, with teams playing twenty-eight games (which is now thirty-four games). The first games tipped off in June of 1997, with the idea of playing their season at a time what wouldn't compete with the NBA, which had playoffs end earlier in the month. The first season, the league drew just over one million fans to 112 season games, or an average of 9,000 fans per game, a number the NBA didn't reach until the twenty-ninth season.

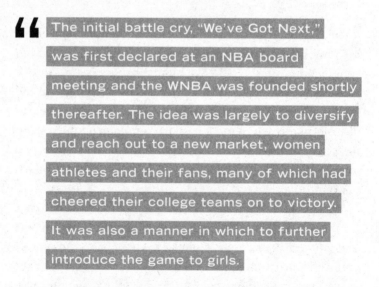

The initial battle cry, "We've Got Next," was first declared at an NBA board meeting and the WNBA was founded shortly thereafter. The idea was largely to diversify and reach out to a new market, women athletes and their fans, many of which had cheered their college teams on to victory. It was also a manner in which to further introduce the game to girls.

Joanne Lannin, author of the book *Finding a Way to Play: The Pioneering Spirit of Women in Basketball*, credits the impetus for getting the league off the ground to the popularity of NCAA women's basketball and the 1996 Olympics. "Following the Gold Medal success of the 1996 USA Women's Olympic team in Atlanta, Georgia, attention was focused on women's basket-ball which made it a great time to start a league. There had been other attempts at a professional women's basketball league, but none had the kind of support and enthusiasm of the WNBA. Players like Sheryl Swoopes, Lisa Leslie, and Re-becca Lobo were the already well-known Olympic stars, and they were ready and excited about playing in the inaugural sea-son of the WNBA,"[1] notes Lannin.

While the initial WNBA teams offered low pay and no mer-chandising revenue for players, it was a starting point for a brand-new league with high hopes. Shortly thereafter, in 1998, the WNBA Players Union was established as the first labor un-ion comprised of professional women athletes.

The WNBA immediately had a competing league with which to contend, the American Basketball League (ABL), which had started play in 1996 as a year-round league. Not unlike the NBA and ABA, there was an immediate war for talent between the two leagues. The WNBA had a significant advantage with finan-cial support from the NBA and television deals in place with NBC and the Walt Disney Company. After just three seasons, the ABL folded in 1999, leaving some players such as Katie Smith, Taj McWilliams, and Delisha Milton-Jones to find a home in the WNBA while others went to play overseas. Unlike adding four teams to the NBA in their 1976 merger with the ABA, players from the now defunct league were on their own and essentially not welcomed into the rival league. In fact, lim-its were placed on how many former ABL players could be on a WNBA roster.

The WNBA, meanwhile, continued forward, celebrating twenty years in 2017; a milestone, considering the cost of running a professional sports franchise. Not unlike the early years of the NBA, the WNBA saw its fair share of teams relocating or folding. In fact, from the original eight teams in 1997 to the current twelve teams, there have been a total of eighteen WNBA franchises.

Only four of the original eight teams remain, including the Utah Starzz, who moved to Las Vegas and became the Aces after a long run in San Antonio. Seven of the current teams are considered sister teams of the closest NBA franchises. The other five teams are owned and run by sponsors, such as the Las Vegas Aces who were purchased by MGM International Resorts and the Connecticut Sun owned by Mohegan Sun, also a major resort and casino.

Finances, Demographics, and Television

The WNBA had been losing money for years. Ten years into the league, teams averaged losing $1.5 to $2 million a season, and overall, the financial losses have not dissipated.

While the WNBA numbers do not match NBA ticket sales, it's all relative to the audience you are attracting. However, two ongoing problems for the WNBA have been getting fair coverage in the male-dominated world of sports reporting and sports talk radio, and determining exactly who makes up the league's demographic market.

"When I was researching my book, I went to many WNBA games as well as women's college games. Since the WNBA games are played during the summer months, with kids out of school, there would be families in attendance along with camp groups, or local teams, mostly girls," Lannin explained about the league demographics. "There were also seniors, looking to relax and get out of the heat. It's hard to get people to come to indoor sports during the summer months. Personally, I think they should have the season start later so it runs into November, where it is only competing with the early part of the NBA season."[2]

Yet, summer games and seasonal competition are only two issues. The question of demographics still persists. The male audience wants the faster pace slam dunking of the NBA, leaving the female audience as the primary market for the WNBA, which was largely anticipated from the start. However, according to a March 2017 HuffPost article, "The WNBA's Biggest Problem Isn't Lack of Interest from Men. It's Women," 75 percent of the WNBA audience are women. Yet, the league is not reaching enough women.

In an essay called "(in)Visibility" written by WNBA star Maya Moore in 2017, and also mentioned in the HuffPost article, Moore wrote: "We need the marketing to match our product. Celebrate us for the things that matter—the stories, the basketball, the character, the fiery competitiveness, our professionalism."[3]

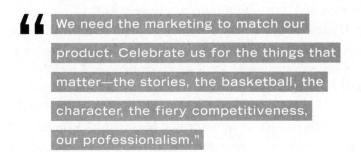

We need the marketing to match our product. Celebrate us for the things that matter—the stories, the basketball, the character, the fiery competitiveness, our professionalism."

"Women will turn out and cheer for the Huskies in Connecticut, or other top college teams because of an allegiance to their schools, but not enough women follow the NCAA stars to the pros nor are they forming a bond with the local professional franchises despite a tremendous level of talent," says Lannin from her researching the WNBA.[4]

Figuring out how to effectively market the league remains a major challenge for team owners and the WNBA in general. To compound the problem is the fact that many of the players (estimated to be more than 60 percent) go overseas to play in other leagues during the off-season to supplement low WNBA salaries. "Diana Taurasi actually sat out an entire season and played overseas where she made a lot more money," explained Lannin. "A lot of players go during the off-season, but she was the first who took an offer to play and opted out of the WNBA season. Obviously, it hurts the league when a big-name player goes to play overseas.

"There has also been the concern of injuries," adds Lannin, commenting on one such prominent example. "Breanna Stewart, the league MVP in 2018, went overseas and tore her Achilles tendon, putting her out for the entire 2019 WNBA season. The injury reopened the ongoing discussion about the WNBA paying their players more money so they wouldn't have to play overseas and run the risk of hurting themselves."[5]

While it would appear that money is tight with the league losing as much as $12 million in 2018 alone, there is money coming into the league from sponsorship deals, which have become "fashionable" with players wearing logos and company names on their uniforms, a trend started in 2009 by the Phoenix Mercury. From MGM Resorts, to banks, GEICO, hospitals and even the Mayo Clinic, the league has utilized these sponsorship deals to help stay afloat. There have also been a number of other sponsorship deals including those with Nike which provide the WNBA player uniforms.

Players, however, are still looking for a bigger slice of the league revenues. According to Brigitte Yuille, a May 2019 posting on Investopedia.com revealed, "the official maximum WNBA salary for veteran players as of 2018 was $113,500. [This is] quite a bit shy of the massive paydays and endorsement deals of their male counterparts. In fact, mid-level NBA players were making $5 million to $10 million a year, with the top players raking in $26 to $30 million."[6]

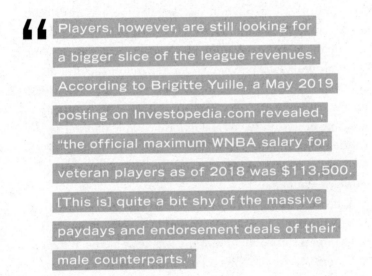

> Players, however, are still looking for a bigger slice of the league revenues. According to Brigitte Yuille, a May 2019 posting on Investopedia.com revealed, "the official maximum WNBA salary for veteran players as of 2018 was $113,500. [This is] quite a bit shy of the massive paydays and endorsement deals of their male counterparts."

The fact that the league is still relatively young provides ongoing optimism for the NBA team owners. Lannin, in a 2017 blog, referred to the comment from former New York Liberty owner and NBA Hall of Famer, Isiah Thomas, when the league hit the twenty-year mark, "The WNBA is actually positioned well when you compare it to the NBA's status after twenty years."[7] Thomas makes a good point. The NBA also did not have an established league helping them grow, nor did it have the sponsorship deals or television coverage that the WNBA has today. The NBA was drawing less than 7,000 per game after twenty years, which is about where the WNBA was as of 2019. The problem for the league is that attendance is going in the wrong direction.

The WNBA teams averaged roughly 10,000 in attendance in 1999, with the New York Liberty leading the charge, topping 14,000, while Phoenix was seeing more than 13,000 in average attendance. By 2009, league average attendance was just over 8,000, with Washington and Los Angeles topping the 10,000 mark and the New York Liberty just under 10,000. Attendance around the league has continued to fall in recent years, leveling off at around 7,000 per game. One reason for the drop in recent years is that the New York Liberty were sold and are no longer owned by the New York Knicks. Therefore, instead of bringing in close to 10,000 at the world-famous Madison Square Garden, they're bringing in just over 2,200 (as of the 2019 season) at the 5,000-seat Westchester County Center, 45-minutes north of Manhattan.

While the falling attendance numbers are of concern to the league, growth can still be achieved by a boost in marketing. Television is still onboard with the league as has been the case all along. Besides the NBC games in the early years, the league also had deals with cable television networks, Lifetime, and Oprah Winfrey's Oxygen Network. ABC, CBS Sports Network, and NBA-TV have all been, and in some cases still are, broadcasting WNBA games, with ESPN also covering games and providing $25 million a year in revenue.

The Product and the Players

The NBA began by selling professional men's basketball as played by the best young pros fresh out of college. They weren't the first league to try to capture basketball fans. The WNBA has taken a similar path, focusing heavily on recruiting players from schools like the University of Connecticut, the power-house of women's basketball for many years. The amazing success of the Connecticut Huskies has drawn significant attention across the sports world and been the source of a lot of WNBA talent including: Rebecca Lobo, Nykesha Sales, Sue Bird, Tamika Williams, Diana Taurasi, Tina Charles, Maya Moore, Stefanie Dolson, and Breanna Stewart, to name a few.

The product offers fans more finesse than the power of the NBA, and features some of the most gifted female athletes in the world, many leading the USA Olympic basketball teams to gold medals. A salary cap and loyalty to teams have helped maintain a competitive balance. Plus, the league has had no shortage of talented stars over the years.

Selling the Product: Women's Basketball

- Point guard Sue Bird was drafted in 2002 by the Seattle Storm. After sixteen years she has now retired. Bird helped lead the Storm to three championships, while leading the league in assists three times and becoming the first WNBA player to appear in over 500 games.
- Tamika Catchings also stayed loyal to the team that drafted her, remaining with Indiana Fever for fifteen years. She won Rookie of the Year in 2002, became the fastest player to reach 2,000 points (in four years), was

voted three-time Defensive Player of the Year and led the league in steals six times. The ten-time All-Star, as of 2019, ranked third all-time in scoring, second all-time in rebounding, and first, by far, in steals.

▪ Brittney Griner is one of the best-known WNBA athletes, largely because of her dunking and blocking abilities. A member of the 2014 WNBA Champion Phoenix Mercury, and part of the USA's 2016 gold medal Olympic team in Rio de Janeiro, Griner has won WNBA Defensive Player of the Year twice during the first seven years of her career.

▪ At 6'6", Lauren Jackson is one was one of the tallest WNBA competitors. She began playing as a teenager in Australian basketball leagues before becoming the top overall WNBA draft pick in 2001. Jackson spent a dozen years playing for Seattle and helped them to two championships, while winning three scoring titles and appearing in seven All-Star games.

▪ Lisa Leslie was the number seven selection in the inaugural WNBA draft and is, as of 2020, the number seven all-time WNBA scorer. The three-time league MVP led the Los Angeles Sparks to two championships while becoming one of the league's all-time top rebounders. But Leslie's career went beyond the WNBA statistics, and even her many Olympic milestones. While moving from player to coach to broadcaster, Leslie became one of the foremost faces of the WNBA.

▪ Sheryl Swoopes is among the most notable names in WNBA history—she entered the league for the inaugural season and was a key part of the four championships of the Houston Comets. She also won two scoring titles before wrapping up her career in Seattle and then Tulsa.

- Tina Thompson had the honor of being the first player selected into the WNBA after starring for four years at USC. She would play a major role in leading the Houston Comets to titles in her first four WNBA seasons. After seventeen years, nine All-Star game appearances, and nearly 500 regular season games, she retired to a coaching position and is now in the Basketball Hall of Fame.
- Diana Turasi, in her fourteen years with the Phoenix Mercury, has won nearly every honor the WNBA and thus far, she has led the team to three titles along the way. The all-time leading scorer to date, and five-time scoring champion, Turasi has also taken time to win an Olympic Gold and play in over 170 games in the Euro-League.

These are just a few of the WNBA standouts over the years. Other notable stars who have played (or are still playing) include: Seimone Augustus, Alana Beard, Rebekkah Brunson, Swin Cash, Tina Charles, Cynthia Cooper-Dyke, Elena Delle Donne, Katie Douglas, Candice Dupree, Yolanda Griffith, Chamique Holdsclaw, Rebecca Lobo, Cheryl Miller (NBA star Reggie Miller's sister), Maya Moore, Nneka Ogwumike, Candace Parker, Cappie Pondexter, Nykesha Sales, Katie Smith, Breanna Stewart, and Teresa Weatherspoon.

Marketing Boost

One of the most significant problems of the WNBA has been the lack of Chamberlain/Russell or Bird/Magic rivalries or omnipresent superstars. This has resulted from a lack of visibility, promotion, and marketing.

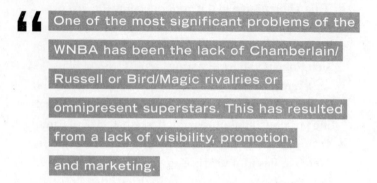

" One of the most significant problems of the WNBA has been the lack of Chamberlain/Russell or Bird/Magic rivalries or omnipresent superstars. This has resulted from a lack of visibility, promotion, and marketing.

When the league started, fresh off the 1996 Olympic Basketball gold medal team, Rebecca Lobo, Sheryl Swoopes, and Lisa Leslie were already well-known names and fans were drawn to see them play. Today, however, outside of the true WNBA fans and followers, few people know the players other than perhaps Brittney Griner, whose dunks make the highlight reels.

As the NBA has demonstrated, individual branding and league brand ambassadors can play a vital role in promoting the league. The theory being that if sports fans familiarize themselves with the players, they'll come to see them in action. This is where the league and publicists have had a major challenge. Positive stories, on and off the court, need more national coverage, such as that of Maya Moore, who put her career on hold (missing a season) to try to get a young man out of jail who she strongly believes is innocent and is wrongfully serving a fifty-year prison sentence. Or Tiffany Jackson-Jones of the L.A. Sparks who "is mostly known for her basketball prowess, but she's also known for beating breast cancer. She decided when she was diagnosed with the disease that she wanted to be a role model for strength,"[8] journalist Lindsey Horsting wrote in an article for WNBA.com.

Also included in the article were Jackson's inspiring words, "I wanted to be an example to everyone, to survivors, to people who are going through the disease, not just basketball players. If I can go back and play basketball, you can go back to your life where you're having fun with your kids, your family, traveling, or whatever it is that you love to do."[9]

While it's not easy to build the individual brands, or the league brand, it is what has made a huge difference in the success of sports leagues, most prominently the NBA. Marketing and branding means being wherever the media is, and being part of social media conversations. It means focusing on the players, and their stories, on and off the court, rather than on team logos or league catchphrases. This would help the WNBA generate more interest from their top demographic audience, women.

Thus far, the jolt the WNBA needs to boost it to a profitable level has not yet happened, which isn't to say it won't. Consider the impact the Williams sisters have had upon women's tennis, raising the bar, and the sport significantly. The same could happen for the WNBA.

There is optimism from WNBA leadership. WNBA Commissioner Cathy Engelbert, (who took the post in July of 2019) was quoted in *Forbes*, saying, "We've got to get the financial metrics and the business models right."[10] Having become the first female CEO of a top four financial firm (Deloitte), Engelbert is determined to make an economic overhaul.

Mark Tatum, deputy commissioner of the NBA who served as interim WNBA commissioner prior to Engelbert's arrival also adds a note of optimism and determination. Tatum told *Forbes* "The goal is that we will turn the WNBA into a self-sufficient business."[11]

"I can accept failure, everyone fails at something. But I can't accept not trying."

—MICHAEL JORDAN

CHAPTER SIX

GOING GLOBAL

Little did Italian born, Canadian raised Henry Biasatti know, when he played six games for the Toronto Huskies in the 1946–47 season, that he would be way ahead of his time as the first of many international players in what was soon to become the NBA.

Fast forward to 2019—more than 100 international athletes from more than forty countries have played in the NBA, and the Toronto Raptors became the first team in league history to play outside the United States and walk away with the championship trophy. Thanks largely to the NBA's global approach to marketing, basketball is now one of the world's most-popular sports, second only to soccer.

In fact, just prior to the 2018 season, in an article for AP News, basketball writer Tim Reynolds quoted NBA Commissioner Adam Silver: "I believe we can be the No. 1 sport in the world. When I look at the trajectory of growth, the fact that young people, boys and girls, continue to love this sport, are playing this sport, are engaged in the sport of basketball on social media or with online games, I don't know what the limit is."[1]

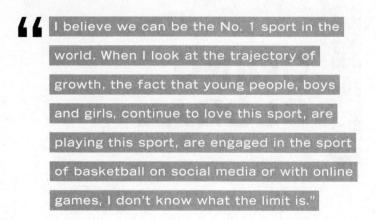

> I believe we can be the No. 1 sport in the world. When I look at the trajectory of growth, the fact that young people, boys and girls, continue to love this sport, are playing this sport, are engaged in the sport of basketball on social media or with online games, I don't know what the limit is."

Reynolds added some numbers to support Silver's statement. "The numbers touted by the NBA are impressive: 300 million people playing the game for fun in China alone, rapid growth in India over the past decade as that country is on pace to become the world's most populous by 2025, an estimated 1 billion people around the globe—that's basically one out of every seven people alive—having some access to the NBA Finals,"[2] wrote Reynolds.

The NBA's international popularity is not brand-new. Much of the initial global impact on the game began in the 1980s and continued to grow throughout the '90s. Nigerian born Hakeem Olajuwon was the top draft pick in 1984 from the University of Houston and went on to win two championships with the Houston Rockets during his Hall of Fame career. Croatian born Dražen Petrović, a European basketball star, brought his skills to the NBA in 1989. There was also four-time NBA Defensive

Player of the Year, Dikembe Mutombo who came to the United States from Léopoldville in the Dominican Republic in 1991.

"It wasn't easy for the first players who came into the league from overseas," says Senior Vice President of International Basketball Operations for the NBA Kim Bohuny. "There were a few players from Eastern Europe who came into the league in the late 1980s, and a few Western European players who had gone to college in the United States, like Detlef Schrempf (from Germany), who went to college at the University of Washington and Rik Smits (from the Netherlands) who went to Marist College in Poughkeepsie, New York," recalls Bohuny.[3]

"The hard part for the players coming in during the late '80s and most of the '90s was that most of them didn't speak English, they also hadn't lived abroad. They didn't see many NBA games because the only way to see the game was on television, and there were not that many games broadcast overseas. Sometimes they would see edited highlight packages or pick up a game in the middle of the night. But there was little to choose from, so they didn't know the players very well nor did they know the style of play,"[4] adds Bohuny, of the pioneering players who came into the NBA from overseas basketball.

In a 2018 *Sports Illustrated* article, Bohuny recounted a story about Manute Bol, who came to America from Sudan. The story, as told to her by former Baltimore Bullets star Wes Unseld, was that the team had found Bol a house and he had moved in. "The next day he doesn't come to practice. So, [his teammates] go to the house and say, 'Are you OK?' He'd never been in cold weather before, and he had a runny nose. He thought he was, like, gravely ill," explained Unseld to Bohuny.[5]

Global Marketing and the NBA

The best way to promote the league abroad was to take games overseas so people around the world could get a feel for the excitement that was the NBA product. As far back as 1978, the Washington Bullets and the Maccabi Tel Aviv met for an exhibition game in Tel Aviv, Israel, where the Maccabi won 98–97.

Over time, exhibition games began to make their way around the world. In 1990, the Phoenix Suns and Utah Jazz played a two-game series in Tokyo, opening the door for the league to take regular season games to other parts of the world. Since that monumental series, typically two games a year have been played abroad, in places like Taipei, Beijing, Shanghai, Rio de Janiero, Mexico City, Paris, London, and Milan.

In the 1990s, under Stern, an effort began to facilitate international interest in the league. The NBA opened offices in various parts of the world. "Think Global, Act Local" was the approach. As such, the NBA wanted to have a presence abroad, but become familiar with the local culture and customs.

In the 1990s, under Stern, an effort began to facilitate international interest in the league. The NBA opened offices in various parts of the world. "Think Global, Act Local" was the approach. As such, the NBA wanted to have a presence abroad, but become familiar with the local culture and customs.

Today there are a dozen offices around the world in major cities including Hong Kong, Toronto, Beijing, Shanghai, Taipei, London, Madrid, Mumbai, Mexico City, Rio de Janeiro, and Johannesburg. Having a presence in such different parts of the world helped grow the business of the NBA, through merchandising, marketing, community events, and so forth. Regional licensing and even international television deals were also coordinated.

But the presence of the NBA abroad wasn't strictly about business opportunities. After all, it still came down to a game that kids loved to play and enjoyed watching. Opportunities to work with children on playing basketball, as well as helping their communities with education and social needs would also become a large part of the NBA's international presence.

The Dream Team

It was the ultimate global introduction to the majesty of the NBA. For the first time, the best of the best would assemble in one place to put their incredible talents on display, for the United States Olympic team, in front of the world. It was truly something special.

For years controversies surrounded the inclusion of professional athletes at the Olympics. The concern was heightened when Eastern European countries, such as Russia and East Germany, introduced state-sponsored amateur athletes. Then, in 1986, the International Olympic Committee voted to allow professional athletes into the Olympic games.

Yet, the 1988 USA Olympic team was made up of college athletes, since the International Basketball Federation (FIBA), the governing body for basketball worldwide, maintained that amateur basketball players should still participate in the Olympics. The issue of players from several nations being paid to play became a hot button, since, despite years of experience, these athletes were still considered amateurs. Nonetheless, despite the difference in age and experience, the US team garnered a bronze medal in 1988 led by future NBAers Dan Majerle, David Robinson, Stacey Augmon, and Mitch Richmond.

The following year, the FIBA made the decision to let professional basketball players compete in the Olympics and the dream began. For the next three years, David Stern led the way with millions of NBA fans forecasting how great a team from the United States would be at the 1992 Olympics.

In Barcelona, the forecasting became a reality as one of the greatest teams the sports world had ever assembled took the court in Barcelona for the 1992 Olympics. The Dream Team, as they came to be known, included Michael Jordan, Magic Johnson, Larry Bird, Charles Barkley, Patrick Ewing, David Robinson, Karl Malone, and John Stockton, among others.

Not only did the team demolish the competition on their way to a gold medal, but they emerged as global superstars. These were the players the NBA showcased worldwide. As Magic Johnson said, "The Dream Team made basketball the game it is around the world."[6]

To a degree Magic Johnson was right. This was at the time when the international love of the game was beginning to take shape and it elevated the players and the league to new heights. Children in far-reaching parts of the world were wearing Dream Team shirts, caps, or other items. The merchandising of Dream Team jerseys, jackets, caps, and T-shirts resulted in millions of dollars in revenue, as well as driving TV ratings up from the previous summer Olympics of 1988.

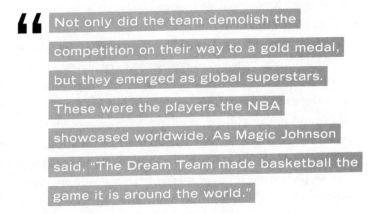

" Not only did the team demolish the competition on their way to a gold medal, but they emerged as global superstars. These were the players the NBA showcased worldwide. As Magic Johnson said, "The Dream Team made basketball the game it is around the world."

American sports had never had this kind of international exposure. In fact, most businesses, other than McDonalds, had never reached a young audience of this proportion, and since it was all part of the Olympics, the NBA could reap the benefits without having to do much heavy lifting. The key, however, was to maintain the enthusiasm and Stern was always thinking one step ahead and ready with new plans to promote business around the globe.

The Next Surge

Once the gates were open, more and more players from around the globe began finding their way to the NBA. It was not an easy task to make it into the most prestigious basketball league in the world. It meant being talented, the best among your countrymen, showing that you could play against top competitors and being seen by NBA scouts. While the Dream Team made headlines, players from many countries were also seen in various worldwide leagues as well as international tournaments, some of whom played their way into the NBA.

After working with the Atlanta Hawks on their Soviet tour in 1989, Kim Bohuny began assisting international players in their transition into the United States. In doing so, she transformed the manner in which players assimilated to life off the court and into American culture. It all got a little easier after the Dream Team introduced basketball to more of the world.

Through the 1990s and into the early 2000s, players came from an increasing number of countries. Steve Nash came south from Canada to join the NBA where he would spend most of his eighteen seasons on the Phoenix Suns as one of the greatest playmakers in the history of the league. The two-time NBA MVP, and eight-time All-Star won five assist titles on his way to over 10,000 career assists.

■ OTHER 1990S INTERNATIONAL STARS:

- ■ Croatian-born Toni Kukoč was one of the first European stars to join the NBA as part of three championship teams with Jordan and the Bulls after holding down the fort for a couple of years while Jordan played baseball.

- ■ Vlade Divac came from Serbia to play for the Lakers, where he was part of two championship teams. He later became general manager of the Sacramento Kings.

- ■ Quiet, likable Dirk Nowitzki, left his native Germany to join the Dallas Mavericks for what remained of the lockout-shortened 1998–99 season and then stuck around with the team for an amazing twenty-one seasons. Dirk played in thirteen All-Star games and led the Mavericks to their only world championship.

- **Tony Parker was one of the few stars to make it to the NBA from France. Parker joined San Antonio in 2001, and played seventeen seasons for the Spurs before wrapping up his All-Star career with a year in Charlotte. He was the quarterback of four Spurs championship teams.**
- **Manu Ginóbili, Parker's long-standing teammate, was also an international star that played professionally in his home country of Argentina, and in Italy. He joined the Spurs for the 2000–01 season on his way to a sixteen-year NBA career, which included four titles.**

North of the Border Expansion

On November 14, 1993, the Canadian Broadcasting Company (CBC) aired segments from a press conference announcing the expansion. Notes from the press conference read as follows:

> "We're going to make the NBA proud. We respect the trust that they've charged us with," says John Bitove, Jr., president of the yet-to-be-named professional basketball franchise in Toronto. NBA commissioner David Stern is on hand to announce the granting of the franchise, as is Jerry Colangelo from the NBA expansion committee. Former premier of Ontario David Peterson is along as well. The price tag for the team is a hefty $125 million US, but Stern notes that in exchange fans will get to see something special. "What we represent is a very high level of family entertainment."[7]

Three separate groups were all bidding to bring a team to Toronto, which had a team (the Huskies) for what was considered the first NBA season of 1946–47. The Huskies folded after that one season. Exhibition games in Toronto, in 1989 and 1992, each drew over 25,000 people and gave credibility to the argument that the city was more than ready to have a team once again. The Raptors began play in the 1995–96 season.

It was also in 1993 that the owner of the Vancouver Canucks of the NHL announced plans to bring an NBA team to the city. There was a 20,000-seat arena already being built which would house both professional teams, as is the case in many major cities. By the spring of 1994, the Vancouver Grizzlies were a done deal at a franchise fee of $125 million, over $92 million more than the expansion teams of the late 1980s.

Despite the growth of the NBA, the Grizzlies lasted six seasons in Vancouver before moving to Memphis. Unfortunately, the novelty of a new team and a new sport in the Vancouver had worn off and attendance dropped significantly. One of the problems the Grizzlies faced was the inability to attract free agents.

And Then Came Yao Ming

By the start of the new century, the NBA had emerged as a global business more than any other professional sports league. The eyes and ears of the league were everywhere, including China, where basketball had been popular for many years. In fact, China had an Olympic team as far back as the 1930s. The NBA first appeared in China in the 1980s when David Stern realized the untapped marketing potential and made a deal with CCTV (the state-run television network) to broadcast NBA games. However, the Chinese Basketball Association (CBA) was not formed until 1995 where, two years later, 7'6" Yao Ming began his career on the Shanghai Sharks and was seen by the NBA.

In 2002, Ming became the first international player to be selected first overall in the NBA draft without having played college basketball in the United States. Ming went on to have an All-Star career for seven seasons before foot injuries ended his career prematurely. But that was only part of the legacy that is Yao Ming. In 2004, Ming and the Rockets would become the first NBA team to play in China, where they played two exhibition games before packed houses. Ming, already a celebrity in China, rose in stature as no basketball player had done before. "Walking around China with Yao Ming is like walking through New York with the Beatles," said former Rockets general manager Carroll Dawson.[8]

> " Walking around China with Yao Ming is like walking through New York with the Beatles."

For the NBA and basketball fans of China, Yao Ming was just the start of things to come. The NBA not only continued playing preseason games in four different cities in China, but in 2016, the league announced the development of elite training centers in Urumqi, Jinan, and Hangzhou. NBA marketing and merchandising also took off in China, which is now the second biggest market for the NBA behind North America. Along with Ming, NBA players, particularly Kobe Bryant, have been largely responsible for the NBA explosion in China, along with the marketing power of major sportswear companies selling signature shoes. Bryant, who rivals Ming's popularity in China, also created a China fund and donated five million yuan (roughly $700,000) to the Sichuan Province that was rocked by a devastating earthquake.

While David Stern opened the door to China, Yao Ming walked through it as an ambassador. The television deal also proved highly lucrative not only for the NBA but for the advertisers sending their brands into a difficult-to-reach market.

Among the recent NBA business agreements with China is a significant deal with Tencent, the parent company of WeChat, the social media, messaging, and payment app. The agreement is to carry games and highlights. In another tech deal the NBA teamed up with the popular Chinese microblogging platform Weibo to deliver NBA game highlights, player interviews, photos, stats, and behind-the-scene events to the 400+ million monthly active users.

Meanwhile, Ming has gone on from his basketball career to represent numerous companies in commercials while also running a variety of businesses from his own wine company in Napa Valley to a private equity fund called Yao Capital. He remains active in the basketball world as president of the Chinese Basketball Association. Ming's presence, in conjunction with the NBA, also helped establish Yao's Charity Game, the NBA China Organization (founded in 2008), NBA Cares events, and the inclusion of Basketball Without Borders inclusion in China.

■ EXPORTS

It should be noted that players not only come from abroad to play in the NBA, but a number of players have taken their game to other parts of the globe for any number of reasons. Some have improved their skills while others wanted a different setting and some got major deals that surpassed their NBA offers at the time. Among those who played in the CBA are Stephon Marbury, Tracy McGrady, and Gilbert Arenas. One of the unintended consequences of such player moves was further promoting the talent of the NBA around the world. It's unintended in that the league does not send players overseas to play, but instead some opt to joining the ever-growing number of competitive leagues abroad.

The Influx of International Players Continues

In the new century, players kept on coming from around the globe.

- European star seven-footer Pau Gasol, came from Barcelona, Spain, and joined the Memphis Grizzlies in 2001. During his twenty-year career, he topped 20,000 points and was part of two championship Lakers teams.
- Pau's brother Marc, also a Spanish basketball star, joined Memphis in 2008 and later won a title with the Raptors in 2019.
- Giannis Sina Ougko Antetokounmpo, the 2018–19 MVP, came to the States from Greece. Sporting the nickname "the Greek Freak," Giannis made his NBA debut at the age of eighteen for the Milwaukee Bucks, and by his third season had established himself as one of the premier superstars in the league.
- Two of the most significant stars of the future, Joel Embiid and Ben Simmons, play for the Philadelphia 76ers. Embiid, a seven-footer from Cameroon, struggled through two years of injuries after being picked third in the 2014 college draft before emerging as a top scorer and rebounder. Ben Simmons, from Australia,

was the first overall pick in the 2016 college draft, and has also emerged as one of the league's most exciting young stars.

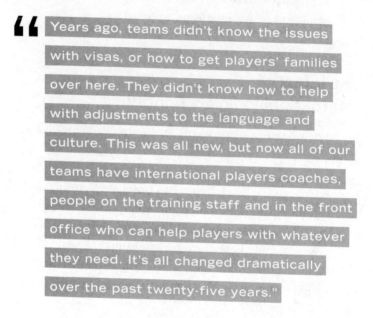

" Years ago, teams didn't know the issues with visas, or how to get players' families over here. They didn't know how to help with adjustments to the language and culture. This was all new, but now all of our teams have international players coaches, people on the training staff and in the front office who can help players with whatever they need. It's all changed dramatically over the past twenty-five years."

Over the years, it has become much easier for players to transition to the NBA and adjust to life in America. Kim Bohuny notes, "Everything is so different for players coming into the league today. First and foremost, they can watch any games they want online, even clips of a particular player playing multiple games if they choose, there is so much material online now . . . there's nothing new when they come here. They also speak English because it's the language of basketball; all of the players know that if you make it into the NBA, the G League, or even the EuroLeague the language will be English so most players are fluent in English. They've traveled all over the world and most have been to the United States before, many taking part in basketball camps, so the transition to the United States and into the league is a lot easier."[9]

Bohuny, who has worked in her position in the NBA for nearly thirty years, adds that teams are also used to having international players on their rosters, so they are prepared. "Years ago, teams didn't know the issues with visas, or how to get players' families over here. They didn't know how to help with adjustments to the language and culture. This was all new, but now all of our teams have international players coaches, people on the training staff and in the front office who can help players with whatever they need. It's all changed dramatically over the past twenty-five years."

TRULY GLOBAL CHAMPIONS

Consider that the 2018–29 NBA Champion Raptors, who play in Toronto, were largely constructed by English-born Nigerian Masai Ujiri, and includes players and coaches from Spain, Cameroon, Republic of the Congo, St. Lucia, and Italy.

It was also a year in which the league MVP was from Greece.

Basketball Without Borders

Among several NBA grassroots and elite development programs, one of the most widely respected is Basketball Without Borders (BWB), which is organized and run in conjunction with the FIBA. Established in 2001, BWB serves as a basketball developmental program that brings high-level young players together to learn and play the game in a supportive environment.

Top young players from Asia, Europe, Latin America, and Africa are selected by the NBA, FIBA, and various international federations to attend what is essentially a mini basketball camp with some significant counselors, or in this case, trainers, including NBA and WNBA players and coaches. While somewhat awestruck to be learning from some of the world's best players, the atmosphere is one of excitement and camaraderie as attendees play completive ball with other top up and coming global talent.

BWB has emerged as a place to find future NBAers. "Luc Mbah a Moute was in our first camp, in Africa," recalls Kim Bohuny, "He was from Cameroon, went to UCLA and on to the NBA. The story of Joel Embiid was that we had reached out to Luc and asked him if, when he ran a camp in Africa, he would let us know who the best players were. Most of our international players go home and do a camp, so if they see great international talent, they can let us know. It turned out that Luc let us know about a player named Joel Embiid who ended up at his camp, so he contacted us and told us immediately about Joel.

"The same thing happened with Pascal [Siakim]. A lot of people didn't know about him, but once he got invited to one of our BWB camps, he had an opportunity to be seen by scouts and did very well. Basketball Without Borders has been very successful at finding players. In fact, eight of the sixty players selected in the 2019 draft were players from Basketball without Borders," explains Bohuny.[10]

"Some of the players were known before they got there, but there were others who came to the camp and excelled, so they went on to careers that they otherwise may not have had," adds Bohuny.[11]

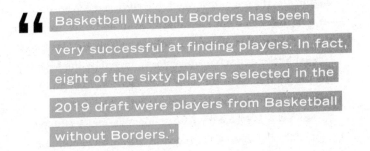

" Basketball Without Borders has been very successful at finding players. In fact, eight of the sixty players selected in the 2019 draft were players from Basketball without Borders."

As the camps and other programs, like the seven NBA basketball academies, generate interest and develop more talent, the league continues to expand its international reach. Teams now have their own scouts in Europe, while many have scouts in Africa, Latin America, and Asia as well.

As for BWB, the international program has included over 3,400 young athletes from more than 120 countries on six continents. It has made a difference for the participants, some in a huge way. Basketball Without Border camps have taken place in cities in five continents, including Europe where Pau Gasol and Danilo Gallinari gained attention that led to their European success and later to their days in the NBA. As of 2020, nearly seventy BWB attendees have been drafted into the NBA or signed as free agents.

BASKETBALL SCHOOLS AND ACADEMIES

While they don't offer official degrees, the NBA also runs basketball schools for boys and girls from the ages of six to eighteen. Located in Brazil, Greece, India, Turkey, and the United Arab Emirates, the schools offer development programs in a similar manner of those run by Basketball Without Borders, with NBA coaches and former players as instructors. The major difference, however, is these are not on a try-out basis but are tuition based and open to all those interested in attending until they fill up. Headed by trained basketball school coaches approved by the NBA, the program teaches on-court skills along with strength and conditioning exercises and basketball education.

At an elite level are the NBA Academies, which employ a holistic, 360-degree approach to player development. The program focuses on education, leadership, health and wellness, character development, and life skills, including educational development for top male and female prospects from outside the United States.

NBA-level coaching also helps emerging talent develop their skills, along with taking part in competitive games. Players may be selected for travel teams that take part in international tournaments. A number of graduates of the international academies have made their way into NCAA D-1 schools, while Han Xu, who trained at the NBA Academy Shandong, was drafted fourteenth overall by the New York Liberty of the WNBA.

Schools and academies provide worldwide training and education for youngsters interested in playing the game. They also promote the NBA as a league and their commitment to education both on and off the court. As a result, it's a win-win situation for the NBA and the attendees.

The Global Business of Basketball in Retrospect

Opening offices around the globe enabled the NBA to make deals abroad with broadcasting companies and other industries, while learning about the cultures, customs, and interests of the people in many nations. Television deals brought basketball to many countries familiar with the game, but not played at the highest level. A host of NBA player-endorsed items, especially shoes, were marketed to countries that were getting to see NBA players in action on television. Then came the Dream Team, and its ambassadors of the game, and the world fell in love with the NBA. It took strategic planning, a consistent desire to stay fresh with new ideas, new merchandise, and camps to teach and develop interest in the game. The NBA also knew it was not just about the dollars and cents, but about giving something to people in various parts of the world who needed the support of a successful business.

NBA Cares, the league's global outreach program, along with Basketball Without Borders united communities around the game while NBA tours, exhibition games, and regular season games kept the focus on the players and the league.

Partnerships have also stretched the boundaries, thanks largely to technology. For example, along with other the China partnerships, the league had also partnered with ByteDance, which offers content programs worldwide—in this case featuring short-form content designed for the NBA audience and available on mobile devices.

Kim Bohuny, who has enjoyed her nearly three decades watching and helping to lead the migration of international athletes into the NBA, still marvels at the global impact the league has had. "I still find it amazing; we see kids with NBA jerseys on all the time, all over the world. It's the number two sport in the world and it's still growing. We see the merchandise and you see kids watching our games on their phones or on their laptops—it is truly incredible to see the reach of the NBA brand around the world," concludes Bohuny.[12]

"You can't get much done in life if you only work on the days when you feel good."

—JERRY WEST

CHAPTER SEVEN

SHUTTING THE BUSINESS DOWN

The Lockout of 1998–1999

From so many perspectives, the 1990s was a great decade for the NBA, led by MJ and six championships for the Chicago Bulls, who had never won a title since their 1966 entry into the league. Globally, the NBA was just hitting its stride with players coming from around the world and a growing fan base from as nearby as Canada and as far away as China. The WNBA brought women's basketball to television and, as the decade neared an end, the average NBA player's annual salary was topping the $2.5 million mark. NBA attendance totals for the 1997–98 season topped 20,000,000 for the third consecutive year, enjoying the second highest total in league history at 20,352,157.

Yet, there was discontent brewing between the players union and the team owners, and while there had been pre-season lockouts before, this was the first time such discontent would manifest itself in a work shutdown. Unlike most businesses in which labor issues are between two parties, management and labor, the NBA has the extra component of being a franchise system. So, while management, aka franchise owners, and players, aka labor, were at either side of the dispute, the league served as the representative for the franchise owners. An extra party in all of this would be the sports agents who, like never before, had a growing interest in the business interests of their clients (the players).

An actual lockout was uncharted territory for the NBA which, unlike Major League Baseball in which a work stoppage went so far as to cancel the 1994 World Series. NBA referees had gone on strike in 1995, but games continued to be played with replacement referees filling the void. Yet, the 1998–99 season would end the harmony. The season would be shut down for 204 days as owners and players drew their own lines in the sand and negotiations in boardrooms replaced action on the hardwood.

Needless to say, the fans and much of the media were not happy, nor were they taking sides, citing the fact a feud between owners and players was hurting the people who enjoy watching the game and those who have jobs in, or related to, the league or the individual franchises. There simply wasn't much empathy from the fans or the sportswriters. In fact, one newspaper columnist called it a feud between tall millionaires and short millionaires. Such sentiments were widely echoed all across the media.

Even those in the broadcast booths were getting edgy as the lockout approached. "It sure doesn't feel good," said former Baltimore, then Washington, Bullets backcourt star, Phil Chenier, a Washington Wizards TV broadcaster and the dean of student life at Howard County Community College.

"Basketball has a nice fall-to-summer cycle to it. That cycle is supposed to be starting now and it isn't. I'm getting edgy,"[1] wrote Jefferson Morley, of the *Washington Post,* about his conversation with Chenier.

Prior to the Lockout

The lockout of 1998–99 didn't appear out of nowhere. There had been a number of issues that had nearly caused lockouts in previous seasons, all of which were settled without the loss of games. Nonetheless, some of the issues remained simmering on a low flame would finally erupt as the negotiations intensified prior to the lockout.

Back in 1983, the NBA had included the first salary cap in professional sports in their Collective Bargaining Agreement and the players got a revenue guarantee of 53 percent. Technically, the league began with a salary cap, but it disappeared after one year. In the 1983 and 1988 negotiations both sides scored points and won on some of the issues that they wanted. Everything went along smoothly with the 1988 negotiations under Charles Grantham, who had been an executive in the NBPA since 1976 and had just taken over the role of executive director. Grantham played a role in four CBA negotiations over fifteen years, during which time the union grew in stature. He was involved in initiating a free agency system that allowed players to negotiate freely with other teams based on the player's years of service. He also started an orientation program for rookies to prepare players for the intense schedule that awaited them in the NBA.

It was in 1994, that Grantham wanted to eliminate three provisions from the previous contract. First was the salary cap, which had been enacted eleven years earlier. Then there was the issue of allowing free agents to negotiate with other teams without the player's team being able to retain the player if they matched the other team's offer. Finally, there was the elimination of the college draft, which had been part of the NBA since the beginning, and has, in more recent years, become a major league event.

The union was unable to win these provisions in negotiations, and the players played the 1994–95 season without a new contract. The union would later lose the battle in court when Southern District Court Judge Kevin Duffy ruled against the players. This meant negotiations would continue, except Grantham resigned and the former deputy commissioner for the league, Simon Gourdine took over. He had already enjoyed a long career in the NBA as assistant to commissioner J. Walter Kennedy and was well versed in negotiations from working as commissioner. In fact, when Kennedy resigned in 1975, there was widespread speculation that Gourdine, second in command, might become the next NBA commissioner and the first African American commissioner in a major sports league. A January 1975 *Ebony* magazine article entitled, "The Best of All Worlds for a Black Pro," highlighted the possibility for such a ground-breaking appointment: "The NBA began its twenty-sixth campaign in October, with some 215 players, approximately 132 (61 percent) of whom are black. Five of the league's 18 franchises have black head coaches . . . and two clubs [have] black general managers. The NBA also employs the highest-ranking black administrator in professional sports. On November 12, 1974, thirty-four-year-old Simon P. Gourdine, a former U.S. Attorney, was elected deputy commissioner of the NBA. Commissioner Walter Kennedy is retiring June 1, 1975, and it is conceivable that when the NBA Board of Governors elects his replacement (possible in January) its choice will be Simon P. Gourdine."[2]

As it turned out, the *somewhat conservative* NBA owners passed over Gourdine for Larry O'Brien, who had political experience, but no prior experience with the NBA. Gourdine stuck around and worked under O'Brien for six years before leaving the league to become the commissioner of consumer affairs under Mayor Ed Koch, the deputy police commissioner and the chairman of New York City's civil service commission. It was in 1990, that he would return to the NBA on the other side of the table. He became the executive director of the players union in 1995, where he negotiated a long-term-bargaining agreement that would remain in place until 1998.

Gourdine Moves On

Gourdine, however, did not remain at the position, as players did not feel comfortable with someone who had been in management taking on their fight. Gourdine would be replaced by former NBA player Alex English and then by Billy Hunter, a former NFL kick returner, who spent sixteen years as the head of the NBPA and found himself in the heat of the 1998–99 lockout. Hunter had left the gridiron for law school and became an attorney who took on some major cases, prosecuting the Hells Angels and the Black Panther Party in his legal career. Hunter took a much more aggressive approach than Gourdine, rallying the players with statements like, "I will kick his ass if need be," referring to David Stern.[3]

Hunter was determined that he would be the man to get the job done for the players. While he had not been involved with the NBA, he familiarized himself with the situation very quickly. "I remember being in a room with thirty-five players and, for some reason, they seemed to focus on what kind of image I would present to David Stern. I think they felt as though they had been sold out in the past. I told them that they didn't have to worry about that with me,"[4] said Hunter in the course of learning more about the ongoing entanglements between the players and the owners.

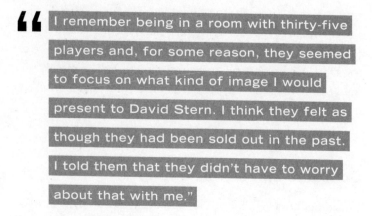

" I remember being in a room with thirty-five players and, for some reason, they seemed to focus on what kind of image I would present to David Stern. I think they felt as though they had been sold out in the past. I told them that they didn't have to worry about that with me."

In March of 1998, during the 1997–98 season, the team owners of the twenty-nine-team league voted 27–2 to reopen negotiations of the Collective Bargaining Agreement signed at the end of the 1995 season. This was possible because in the 1995 agreement it stated that such negotiations could be started if the players had exceeded 51.8 percent of league revenue, which they had done, clocking in with nearly 57 percent of the league's $1.7 billion in league revenue. Over three months, there were several negotiations with little accomplished. One of the most significant points of contention was the salary cap, which came into existence in 1983. This was always a point of contention for players, but the franchise owners needed such a salary cap to curtail runaway salaries, and small market teams needed it to stay competitive.

On May 27, 1998, the owners made a proposal that included the elimination of the Larry Bird exception, as well as a provision no player would be allowed to earn more than 30 percent of a team's total salary cap, which would be a hard salary cap, without the many exceptions that made the salary cap easy to circumvent. (The Larry Bird exception was enacted to help teams hold onto their star players, which was the case of Bird and the Celtics, whereby if the player re-signed with his current team, that player's salary was not counted against the salary cap. This enabled owners to sign their top players and use the extra cap space to sign another player.) While the owners liked this exemption, the union did not. The rookie pay scale and league minimum salaries were also on the table and up for renegotiation. It was $272,000 at the time of the lockout. An individual player salary cap was to be set at a maximum of $10 million per year. Shortly thereafter, the NBPA rejected the deal making it clear that the two sides were far apart. Then, in late June the franchise owners voted 27–2 in favor of a lockout. There had been lockouts before, but none had ever impacted upon an NBA season. This time the sides were not just far apart, but more adamant in their positions.

The 1995 CBA never really sat well with either side—it was one of those agreements that kept the games going on while leaving many unfinished agenda items on the table.

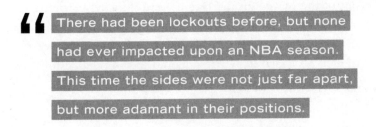

There had been lockouts before, but none had ever impacted upon an NBA season. This time the sides were not just far apart, but more adamant in their positions.

As is often the case in a dispute between labor and management, money was at the top of the list. Spiraling salaries began in the days of the NBA-ABA battle for players. However, over the years they continued to increase at a staggering rate. The average NBA player was making $35,000 in 1970 but by 1977, it was $130,000, a jump of nearly 380 percent with the Laker's Kareem Abdul-Jabbar topping the all salaries with $625,000 per year.

Some twenty years later, Kevin Garnett, who was a one-year-old when Kareem topped the league with his huge salary, signed a seven-year contract worth $126 million, or $18 million a year. At the time, the 1997–98 season, the league average salary was already up to $2.96 million. There was also an increasing disparity amongst teams, many of which simply could not afford to pay free agents the astronomical star salaries.

There were a number of other concerns voiced by owners, including lower attendance numbers from several franchises including Charlotte, Dallas, Detroit, Golden State, Portland, Sacramento, Toronto, and Vancouver. There were also concerns by the league, such as a decline in merchandise revenues and a number of negative off-court stories that made headlines involving illegal weapons, domestic abuse, and narcotics which did not represent the league in a good light. It didn't help matters that a 1997 *New York Times* survey stated that 60–70 percent of the players in the league were smoking marijuana.[5] There was even some appalling behavior on the court, particularly in the case of Warriors guard Latrell Sprewell who tied to strangle his coach P.J. Carlesimo and was suspended for the remaining sixty-eight games of the season.

■ **ABOUT THE NBA SALARY CAP**

The NBA salary cap, first introduced in the 1984–85 season, was initially set at $3.6 million, with a percentage of which teams had to spend to assure a competitive balance. The league's salary cap is determined each year as a percentage of league revenues, also known as basketball related income (BRI) which includes ticket sales, broad-casting fees, naming rights, luxury box sales, in-arena advertising, etc. Teams spending more than the salary cap would face a luxury tax which would be distributed amongst franchises to further a balance in the league.

An example of the success of the NBA can be seen in the salary cap for the 2019–20 season, which was set at $109.140 million. The minimum team salary was set at 90 percent of the salary cap, or $98.226 million, for the 2019–20 season.

Issues on the Table

Along with the salary cap concerns was free agency and the Larry Bird exemption which was implemented in 1983.

At the bargaining table was NBA commissioner David Stern, Deputy Commissioner Russell Granik, and legal counsel, Jeffrey Mishkin, all of whom represented the twenty-nine team owners which included individual billionaire owners and large companies such as Turner Entertainment who owned the Atlanta Hawks, and Comcast who owned the Philadelphia 76ers. Billy Hunter, former New York Knicks star, NBPA president Patrick Ewing, and legal counsel Jeffery Kessler were at the table representing the 400+ players.

As the summer began, there was an eerie "calm before the storm" atmosphere around the NBA. "There is nobody in the NBA who thought it would be business as usual coming out of that season," said Bob Whitsitt, then the Portland Trail Blazers' president and general manager. "If someone didn't expect a lockout for at least the summer, they didn't really know what they were doing."[6]

For decades, union and labor issues had resulted in work stoppages in numerous industries. Now, along with the highly paid players and coaches, the staffers at the NBA offices and at the offices of the twenty-nine franchises, along with the many people whose living was based on the activity of busy arenas during the NBA season, were all awaiting their fate come the fall. During the summer, many league and team staffers began the unpleasant task of rethinking their employment options to cover themselves if the lockout actually continued into the season.

The Battle and the Results

There was little league activity, only speculation going on throughout the month of July, while behind closed doors union leaders came up with their own proposal to match up against what the owners were offering. In August, both sides sat down, met, talked about the CBA and the union presented their proposal. The owners got up and left.

Neither side budged throughout the summer and by early October all exhibition games were being cancelled. It was also in early October when Hunter called for a meeting of all union members in Las Vegas. While players had their own ideas about what they wanted, Hunter managed to maintain unity, which was getting strained with the season approaching.

The basketball media, with little else to cover, was following up on gossip and other stories about Hunter, and the many agents who were now getting involved in the lockout. But neither media pundits, nor agents, could sort out the issues dividing the two sides.

By October 8, the first two weeks of the regular season were cancelled after several hours of meetings generated no positive results. A couple of weeks later, a judge ruled in favor of the owners that they did not have to pay off guaranteed contracts during the lockout. After several multi-hour meetings, David Stern regretfully announced, on December 4, 1998, that it was more likely than not that there won't be a season. While meetings continued throughout December, the vast majority of NBA fans had lost interest. The league was shut down, along with the ancillary businesses that it affected.

Finally, a month to the day after Stern's announcement, the union presented a final offer to the owners. By this point the league had issued a "drop dead" date of January 7 at which point the season would be officially cancelled. On January 6, Stern and Hunter met all night and finally ironed out an agreement that ended the lockout.

Part of the season would be salvaged. Games would begin on February 5, 1999. The season would be fifty games followed by playoffs. Many league and team staffers returned to work after making their way through more than six months of the lockout, others preferred to stay put with employment that they had found elsewhere. The website theringer.com may have summed it up best: "The work stoppage was a disaster. With volatile personalities at the forefront and backbiting among players, owners, and agents, the 1998–99 NBA lockout spanned 204 days and resulted in the loss of about $500 million in total player salaries and more than $1 billion overall."[7]

The players' union conceded on a hard cap of defined revenues of 55 percent during years four through six of the agreement and they accepted a limit on individual player salaries. This limit on individual player salaries was a first in major U.S. professional sports leagues and was a loss to agents who looked to run up high salary bidding wars. The players received increases in the minimum salary, with $287,500 for rookies and more for veterans, based on a sliding scale. There were also additional exceptions to the salary cap, including a middle-class exemption, which meant teams could now sign one player a year, outside the cap, at the league's average salary, plus the Larry Bird Exception remained. In what was more of a very costly showdown to see which side blinked first, both sides blinked and, in the end, when the season was on the line, an agreement was reached.

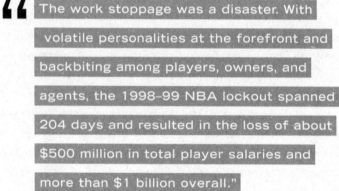

The work stoppage was a disaster. With volatile personalities at the forefront and backbiting among players, owners, and agents, the 1998–99 NBA lockout spanned 204 days and resulted in the loss of about $500 million in total player salaries and more than $1 billion overall."

The Impact

It was widely agreed that the owners fared better than the union by getting the salaries somewhat under control, despite the fact that it came at a cost of $1 billion. The league would continue to have a salary cap, with various exemptions and methods to work around the cap to sign players. This, and the individual salary cap were wins for the league.

While the fans were not pleased, losing three months of games, they came back rather quickly to a fifty-game season. Attendance dropped from just over 17,000 per game to just over 16,700 per game. By 1999–2000, attendance for the season was close to the prior full season.

As for television ratings, they were down for the fifty-game shortened season and for the following three seasons. On a positive note, the shortened season saw the San Antonio Spurs, led by David Robinson and Tim Duncan, become the first former ABA team to win an NBA championship in a five-game series over the New York Knicks. Games one and two were played at the Alamodome and saw a record in NBA finals history topping the 39,500 mark for each game.

From a business standpoint, the NBA handled the lockout carefully, recognizing the value of both side's arguments. While representing the franchise owners' concerns, there was always awareness that the level of talent in the league was not replaceable. Work stoppages represent a tightrope of sorts whereby business owners, and employee representatives need to focus on compromises over their own egos. In the end, Stern and Hunter got the job done, but there was plenty of off-court gamesmanship by owners and players that prolonged the final outcome.

The biggest loss for the league and its fans were not the thirty-two games off each team's schedule, but of Michael Jordan who retired for the second time. He would, however, return a few years later to play again with the Washington Wizards.

"I've got a theory that if you give 100 percent all of the time, somehow things will work out in the end."

—LARRY BIRD

CHAPTER EIGHT

STRONGER THAN EVER

The New Millennium, the Lakers, LeBron, and a Massive TV Deal

It didn't take long for the NBA to rebound from the lockout of 1998–99. The product was still strong and fans were, for the most part, quite forgiving. While television ratings dipped a little during the first few years after the lockout, which was also post-Jordan, the league was ready for the next wave of stars to take the torch that had been passed down from Chamberlain and Russell to Kareem to Bird, Magic, and Jordan. Merchandising and marketing efforts were now international and the plan was to continue presenting NBA action to as many parts of the globe as possible while also continuing to make community outreach a priority. As for the product, it was as strong as ever.

By 2000, the Lakers were in top form led by two new NBA torchbearers, Kobe Bryant and Shaquille O'Neal. They were on their way to the first of three consecutive titles, and the term three-peat became part of sports vocabulary. A major market dynasty in Los Angeles was a great way to tip-off the new millennium, packing the Staples Center with close to 19,000 per game through three championship seasons. The Lakers three-peat also saw the team's revenue jump from just over $150 million to $170 million for the 2001–02 season while Kobe and Shaq became iconic sports personalities on and off the court.

During the first decade of the new millennium, Kobe's impact on the league was huge. Shaq notwithstanding, Kobe became the face of the league, drawing attention everywhere he went. He appeared in the only four NBA finals between 2000 and 2010 to draw double-digit TV ratings which increased the sale of Kobe shirts, jerseys, and other items. There were also increased ticket sales everywhere he went, even in his visits to other countries. Even as other names began to dominate the sport, Kobe could not be ignored. By the end of his twenty-year career with the Lakers, he walked away with a career scoring average of exactly twenty-five points per game, winning two scoring titles and five NBA championships in a Hall of Fame career.

In November of 2015, near the end of Kobe's outstanding career, ESPN senior writer J.A. Adande wrote an article entitled, "Why Kobe Bryant was so important to the NBA," pointing out the impact he had on the exorbitant franchise evaluations, TV, rights and the ever-growing success of the NBA globally. Adande quoted former Lakers general manager Mitch Kupchak who spoke about Kobe: "Our exposure worldwide, the TV deals and the marketing . . . I can't say you can pin it all on Kobe, but certainly when we go from city to city, every building we go into there are three or four thousand Lakers fans there with No. 24 jerseys on, even in the arenas where we're most hated. And to me, he's a universal sports celebrity. Really transcends athletics. How do you quantify that kind of success and how do you relate that to the success of the NBA? I think it goes hand in hand."[1]

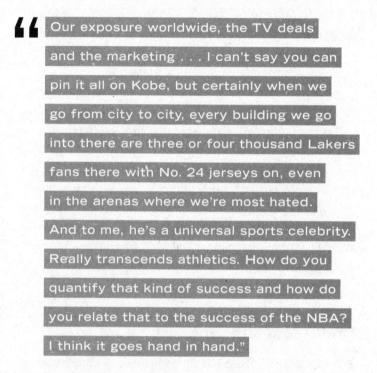

" Our exposure worldwide, the TV deals and the marketing . . . I can't say you can pin it all on Kobe, but certainly when we go from city to city, every building we go into there are three or four thousand Lakers fans there with No. 24 jerseys on, even in the arenas where we're most hated. And to me, he's a universal sports celebrity. Really transcends athletics. How do you quantify that kind of success and how do you relate that to the success of the NBA? I think it goes hand in hand."

As for Shaquille O'Neal, he was one of the greatest centers in NBA history. Yet while Shaq was extremely popular, he was often overlooked when it came down to the best of the best. It was often assumed because of his size and strength, that he had a big advantage, much as Chamberlain had several decades earlier. However, those who've watched the game closely have recognized that many big men who've played in the league did not have the quickness, the passing skills, or the abilities to block 2,700 shots, score 28,000 points, and win four titles. Shaq was unique for his size. The man with the size 22 shoes and a huge personality is in the conversation with the greatest centers of all time, as he should be. Like Kobe, Shaq became an international phenomenon who, after a career as a rapper, is still very much linked to the NBA as an ambassador of the game, seen regularly as a commentator for TNT television.

While the Lakers were on their three-peat run, Michael Jordan decided, at the age of thirty-five, that he wanted to be a part of the action and returned to the NBA, joining the Wizards in 2001, after missing three seasons. Jordan's comeback was welcomed and he was still a 20-point scorer who younger players still had a hard time defending. It goes without saying the presence of Jordan boosted attendance as well. In 2000–01 the Wizards drew just over 638,000 or 15,577 per game. For the two Michael Jordan seasons that followed, attendance was up by over 200,000 to 800,000+ and over 20,000 per game.

Draft Class Supreme

The success of the NBA has always hinged, to some extent, on the annual college draft. What was once limited to the best United States college athletes has now opened up to a global class of young players thanks largely to the league's international presence. While only a few of the thousands of college team players will ever enjoy an NBA career, each draft class helps shape the future of the league.

In 2003, the NBA had one of the most memorable draft classes in NBA history generating headlines well before the start of the 2003–04 season. Led by the Cleveland Cavaliers' first round pick of LeBron James, three of the following four players went on to All-Star careers, Carmelo Anthony, Dwyane Wade, and Chris Bosh. Others in the same draft class include Josh Howard, Kendrick Perkins, and Kyle Korver.

LeBron James had already generated tremendous media attention from his days as a high school star in Akron, Ohio, and not long after entering the league he would supplant Kobe as the face of the NBA. LeBron was soon signing worldwide endorsement deals with Kia, Gatorade, Sprite, Beats, Intel, and Blaze Pizza, along with a $1 billion lifetime deal with Nike. LeBron instantly became his own brand and the new brand ambassador for the league—like Jordan, LeBron became the single-most recognizable, and marketable athlete in the country and perhaps in the world. Clearly the league benefited from all of this with increased revenues from spikes in attendance and merchandising as well as the ancillary revenue from LeBron's notoriety.

For seven years LeBron would play for the Cleveland Cavaliers, single-handedly leading them past the Pistons to their first-ever finals appearance in the 2006–07 season where they lost to the San Antonio Spurs in four games. In 2010, LeBron became a free agent and the sports world got caught up in the drama that followed, so much so that ESPN aired a program in July 2010 called *The Decision*, on which LeBron would announce to the world where he chose to play. While ESPN and LeBron took a lot of criticism for such an over-the-top spectacle, LeBron decided to team up with his two buddies from the 2003 NBA draft, Dwyane Wade and Chris Bosh, to form their own super team in Miami.

While the team boosted league revenue, there was concern throughout the NBA that players forming a super team could potentially set a bad precedent. Owners were concerned about the balance of power being too easily shifted by the player's decisions, some of whom took salary cuts to play together under the salary cap. This could put smaller market teams at a disadvantage.

The new "super team," as expected, went to the NBA finals, and LeBron was anticipating his first championship season.

Dirk Nowitzki and the Dallas Mavericks had other ideas, defeating the Heat in six games, for their first ever NBA title. LeBron and the Heat would capture the next two championships. He then returned to Cleveland for some unfinished business, bringing a title to the team on which it all began.

Setting many league records in an outstanding career, while amassing what is estimated by *Forbes* to be close to half a billion dollars through his NBA career, including the numerous endorsement deals, LeBron is among the NBA's all-time elite, frequently talked about in the same sentence as Michael Jordan.

▪ THE LEBRON FACTOR ON LOCAL BUSINESSES

A July 2, 2018, article by Selena Hill for Blackenterprise .com, written during LeBron James' third free agent decision, in which he chose the Los Angeles Lakers, pointed to a study about the effect of James on the local economy of wherever he signed. The 2017 study, published by the American Enterprise Institute (AEI) quantified the effects that he had in Cleveland with the Cavaliers and his four years with the Miami heat from 2011 to 2014. "The data revealed that James' presence in both of these cities had a huge impact on their local economies by boosting restaurant revenue, ticket sales, and job creation. According to the report, the number of eateries and bars within a mile of the stadium where James was based at the time increased by 13 percent. In turn, employment within those establishments increased by 23.5 percent. While, on the other hand, those numbers dropped when James was not on either team,"[2] wrote Hill.

Highs and Lows

As is the case in any journey, there are high and low points. Financially the league, since 2000, has been extremely success-ful, topping the $3 billion-dollar mark in revenue in the 2003–04 season and by the end of the 2017–18 season had more than doubled that total. According to *Forbes* "the thirty-team league produced $7.4 billion in revenue," which was a 25 percent in-crease from the previous season. By the end of the 2018–19 season the league topped $8 billion in revenues.[3]

There were many highlights, as the NBA continued moving forward with new ideas and an aggressive approach to reaching out nationally and globally. For years the NBA had found ways to turn something big into something bigger, such as taking the All-Star game and turning it into a three-day league celebra-tion. The league also began televising the college draft back in 1980, the same year as the NFL. Then, just prior to the new millennium, the league launched their own TV network, which started in 1999 as the first subscription network run by a pro-fessional sports league in the United States.

NBA TV grew over the next twenty years and now reaches over 50 million households in the United States with original programming and a wide selection of out-of-market games, in-cluding WNBA games on a nightly basis throughout the WNBA season. Continuing to take full advantage of the global popu-larity of the league, NBA TV is now broadcast in forty nations.

Television has always been an integral part of the NBA's mar-keting and revenue stream. In 2016 the league announced the signing of a $24 billion nine-year TV deal with ABC and ESPN (owned by Disney) as well as TNT and NBA TV (both owned by Turner Broadcasting) which went into effect for the 2016–17 season. This brought in league revenue of more than $2.6 billion annually. The new deal saw a 180 percent increase in NBA revenue from the previous deal. Additionally, the deal also led to out-of-market games on broadcast television, continuing to market the sport significantly.

An October 2014 *Sports Illustrated* article quoted NBA Commissioner Adam Silver speaking about the deal. "The Walt Disney Company and Turner Broadcasting share responsibility for the growing popularity and interest the NBA enjoys, and we are thrilled to extend our partnerships," Silver said. "With these new agreements, our fans will continue to benefit from the outstanding NBA coverage and programming provided by ABC, ESPN, TNT, NBA TV and their digital platforms."[4]

The Continuing Growth of the Signature Shoe Market

For many years, network television meant top teams playing in nationally televised games on Sunday afternoons. As a result, fans became familiar with the Celtics, Lakers, and Jordan's Bulls. But other stars remained somewhat anonymous to the casual fan. That has all changed. Today many players have huge followings and have enhanced their personal brands, and subsequently, marketed the NBA, with their own signature-brand shoes.

What began with Air Jordans has morphed into a major rite-of-passage for NBA players. Kobe, Shaq, LeBron James, Steph Curry, James Harden, Kevin Durant, Kyrie Irving, and a number of other top stars are taking it to the feet with deals from major sneaker companies like Nike and Adidas.

In some cases, players are signing with smaller companies that are looking to have an NBA player endorsing their product to help them get on the map. The international impact of the sport has even led players like Dwayne Wade, Klay Thompson, and Rajon Rondo to sign deals with Chinese sneaker companies.

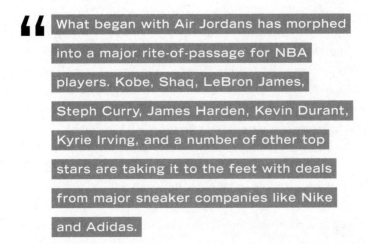

What began with Air Jordans has morphed into a major rite-of-passage for NBA players. Kobe, Shaq, LeBron James, Steph Curry, James Harden, Kevin Durant, Kyrie Irving, and a number of other top stars are taking it to the feet with deals from major sneaker companies like Nike and Adidas.

The sneaker companies are well-aware of the impact NBA players have had on sales and are ready to offer millions of dollars to the next potential superstar. While it's still a gamble, as not all players will dominate the shoe market, there are typically some "sure bets," and the shoe giants are poised to make them. For example, Zion Williamson, within a couple of months of the 2019 NBA draft, which saw the power forward land with the New Orleans Pelicans, signed a multi-year deal $75-million-dollar deal with Jordan Brand, produced by Nike.

While the NBA is not in the business of footwear, the shoe deals provide immeasurable promotion and marketing for the league through its brand ambassadors. This goes back to the benefits of brand ambassadors, especially if they are asked to endorse products to your demographic audience.

Sponsorship

Having surpassed the $1 billion in sponsorship spending for the first time in 2017, topping the MLB but not the NFL, the league continues to seek out more space for sponsors. Part of the recent increase in league sponsorship revenue was attributed to selling a small space on player uniforms in the form of (2.5" by 2.5") patches to advertisers. Based on the success of such advertising in NASCAR and soccer, the league has allowed team uniforms to have a patch with an advertiser's name or logo. Such patches were first introduced into the WNBA in 2009.

Not all NBA teams initially agreed to the idea. In the first season that patches were allowed, 21 teams participated, but with teams bringing in an estimated $6.5 million per year in additional revenue, it was anticipated that all thirty teams would take part in the new sponsorship deals shortly thereafter.

▪ EXPANSION TO CHARLOTTE . . . AGAIN

Only one team joined the NBA during the first two decades of the twenty-first century and that was the Charlotte Bobcats, who became the second team to call Charlotte home. The original Charlotte Hornets moved to New Orleans. The new franchise was called the Bobcats, but after the name of the New Orleans team was changed to the Pelicans, the Charlotte Bobcats took the name back and became the second iteration of the Hornets.

NBA Firsts

Branching out into new territory has become customary for the NBA. It's the mark of a forward-thinking business. They have made strides in each decade, and achieved a lot of firsts in the 2000s and 2010s.

- In 2001, the NBA hired their first female coach, Lisa Boyer, who had the honor of being hired to a coaching position by the Cleveland Cavaliers where she remained for one season. Among the coaches that would follow were the first full-time assistant coach, Becky Hammon who joined Gregg Popovich's staff in 2014 and has remained onboard, and Lisa Gottlieb who became the first women coach recruited from college by the Cleveland Cavaliers in 2019. The NBA also began hiring female referees as far back as 1997.

- In 2005, the NBA launched their first community service program called NBA Cares, designed to address social issues both domestically and globally. Players, former players, and personnel from both NBA and WNBA franchises have since participated in hundreds of community outreach, education, and enrichment initiatives in as many as forty countries. NBA Cares has also partnered on projects with numerous established community-focused organizations including the YMCA, UNICEF, Autism Speaks, Boys and Girls Clubs of America, the Make-A-Wish Foundation, Prevent Child Abuse, the Special Olympics, and the Red Cross, among others. Among other specific NBA Cares programs include NBA Green, Hoops for Troops, NBA Fit, NBA Voices, and Mind Health.

- In 2010, just seven years after his final retirement from the NBA, Michael Jordan purchased controlling ownership in the Charlotte Hornets, becoming the first African American owner of any major professional North American sports franchise. Jordan, although born in the Brooklyn, grew up and went to college in North Carolina giving him an affinity for the state. After enduring nearly a decade of primarily losing seasons, Jordan sold off some of his interest in the team to a couple of Wall Street executives in 2019 to help him steer the franchise in the right direction.

- In 2017, the NBA, always looking for the next great opportunity, signed a deal with Gatorade to sponsor the NBA Developmental, or D-League, which had been around since 2001. The G League, as it is now called, became the first professional pro-sports league to be sponsored by a major brand. While the intent of the D-League was to develop players, the higher visibility of the G League, thanks to Gatorade, will now generate increased media attention and coverage. Sporting twenty-eight teams, the league is already assuming a greater role as a minor league affiliate to NBA teams. While the minimum age in the NBA is nineteen, it's only eighteen in the G League, which provides a place to play for quality players to hone their skills for a year. A number of G League players have made their way onto NBA rosters. While the teams are affiliates of NBA clubs, most players are free agents signed to a G League team, but not an NBA franchise, which makes them available to sign with any NBA team.

THE FIFTH COMMISSIONER

It was anticipated that one day David Stern would step down and that his shoes would be hard to fill. That day came in 2014, when after thirty productive years at the helm, Stern decided it was time to move on with his life. Fortunately, the NBA had groomed a successor who was primed and ready to carry on the legacy of commissioners like Stern and Kennedy. The position went to attorney Adam Silver, who began working for the NBA in 1992 as a special assistant to the commissioner. After serving in several executive roles in the NBA, including deputy commissioner, Silver was elected unanimously by the board of governors to step into the role of NBA commissioner, where he could now utilize his twenty-two years of experience with the league.

Silver's manner of doing business was a lot like that of his predecessor: stay positive, maintain a culture of learning, and consistently embrace new ideas and seek ways to move the league forward.

Under Silver, the owners and players union agreed to a new CBA in 2016, and the 24.1 billion-dollar TV deal was signed. Marketing and league promotions continued to draw fans to arenas nationwide with attendance reaching a new high, topping 22 million for the first time in 2017–18. The result of such revenue numbers has seen the overall franchise values rise dramatically from an estimated $12 billion to $60 billion since Silver took over. Silver has since been given a five-year contract extension.

The Lows

Not everything runs smoothly for any business, including the NBA which has overcome a lot in over seventy years. While the first two decades of the new century included many positives, including new financial highs for teams and players, more televised games, and record highs in attendance, there were a few stains along the way, including an out-of-control brawl that unfortunately became headline news.

It was in November of the 2004–05 season that a game between the Pacers and the Pistons at the Palace of Auburn Hills (home of the Detroit Pistons) turned ugly, in a way never before seen in the NBA. It occurred with less than one-minute remaining on the game clock when the Pacers' forward Ron Artest put a hard foul on Pistons center Ben Wallace, who got incensed and went after Artest with a hard shove. Several players tried to intercede, but some were still angered by the actions of Wallace. Then, as things appeared to be calming down, with Artest, for some reason, lying down on the scorers table, a fan pelted Artest with a beer from close range.

Then, things went from bad to worse, and for the first time in NBA history, the implied barrier between fans and players was broken, as Artest furiously ran into the crowd after the perpetrator. The resulting melee between fans and players was a scary scene. It took security and uniformed police to get the Pacers off the court and into the locker rooms while Pistons' fans threw beer bottles and cups onto the court.

David Stern responded to the brawl as, "shocking, repulsive, and inexcusable—a humiliation for everyone associated with the NBA."[5] Suspensions and heavy fines were then handed out. Six Pacers and four Pistons were suspended—Artest's suspension was for the remainder of the season, while teammate Stephen

Jackson's was for thirty games for following Artest into the stands. Five players later faced criminal charges and ended up doing community service, while five fans were also hit with criminal charges and given lifetime bans from attending Pistons games at the Palace.

Not long after, the NBA addressed security issues, limiting the size and number of drinks sold during games, and cutting off all beer sales after the third quarter. The number of security guards around the teams and the court was also increased league wide.

In 2011, the league faced a second owner lockout which led to a disruption of play. This time Hunter and Stern started verbal jousting in the media before the prior season tipped off. Hunter claimed there was a "99 percent chance of a lockout," while Stern made it clear that he was seeking "a one-third reduction in player salaries, dropping player costs by $750–800 million per season."[6]

Shortly after a successful 2010–11 season, the lockout began. Frustrated, several players started considering the European leagues, the most significant of which was Kobe Bryant, although it may have just been a ploy to step up negotiations, which continued at a standoff, with preseason games being cancelled, just as they were in the prior lockout. This time, however, along with numerous unproductive closed-door meetings, the conflict made its way onto Twitter. For several months there were a lot of conversations but little action by the key parties, as fans, players and owners geared up for what could be a possible repeat of the lockout of 1998–99.

Then, quietly, the lockout was settled in late November, after roughly 150 days. The season was shortened by only sixteen games. The NBA board of governors voted 25–5 to ratify a new ten-year Collective Bargaining Agreement. The 240 missed games dropped the league in attendance below 21 million for the first time in seven seasons, but the average attendance per game dropped only slightly remaining over 17,000. By the following season (2012–13) league numbers were right back where they were in the pre-lockout season.

An extremely regrettable incident that rocked the NBA and came as a shocker to the fans was the gambling scandal involving referee Tim Donaghy. An FBI investigation led to the arrest of Donaghy, who pleaded guilty to conspiracy to engage in wire fraud and transmitting betting information through interstate commerce in a tips-for-payoffs scheme. Donaghy served fifteen months in prison on two concurrent sentences. While Donaghy was first accused of gambling on games in which he was officiated in during the 2006–07 season, it was later reported, when ESPN began doing its own investigative reporting on the story, that he was linked to gambling activities for as many as four previous seasons.

While such betting scandals have appeared in professional and college sports in the past, such as the 1919 Black Socks scandal, the Pete Rose gambling issues, and the point-shaving scandal in college basketball in the 1950s, this was the first incident of this nature in the history of the NBA.

Commissioner David Stern was in disbelief at first, but made it clear that the NBA would cooperate fully with the FBI investigation, which they did. The idea that a referee could, and would, call fouls late in a game to sway the final score by just a few points was hard to believe. It seemed too obvious to actually work. And yet, it did, prompting Stern to take a more aggressive stance with revised NBA referee guidelines and background checks. Also, thanks to improved technology, more video footage is available today than ever before and referees can be more carefully monitored after games in which they have been involved.

As reported by the *New York Times* in a July 2007 press conference, Stern told reporters about the federal investigation and the betting scandal, and the need to uphold the integrity of the sport. "We take our obligation to our fans in this matter very, very seriously. . . . I can tell you that this is the most serious situation and worst situation that I have ever experienced either as a fan of the NBA, a lawyer for the NBA, or a commissioner of the NBA."[7]

While no business can forecast all of the activities that will transpire during the life of the company, the key is how the leaders react to those that are most unexpected. In these situations, the NBA has always made a concerted effort to be transparent in reporting the facts, learn, and make the necessary changes, such as taking security measures to prevent events such as the brawl in the Palace at Auburn Hills, and uphold the league's integrity by taking a deeper look into the hiring of referees for the league. Learning from mistakes and unexpected activities is the best a business can do to move forward.

CONCLUSION

The NBA Today

The NBA is a thriving business and a model of how a sports league can become a global entity with fans and revenue streams worldwide. According to *Forbes*, every individual franchise in the NBA is now worth close to $2 billion dollars, having tripled in a five-year time period.[1] The NBA also stands to remain lockout free for the next several years thanks to a 2017 Collective Bargaining Agreement that will last until the 2023–24 season.

An influx of talent continues to drive the league forward. Merchandising continues to be a billion-dollar revenue stream with jerseys by LeBron James, Stephen Curry, Giannis Antetokounmpo, Kyrie Irving, and Joel Embiid leading the way. While the NBA still benefits from the $24 billion TV deal the league signed with ESPN and TNT, local television contracts bring in anywhere from $120 million to $150 million annually according to Investopedia.com.[2] Cable television, including NBA-TV, plus streaming services make sure that there is a wealth of NBA action available.

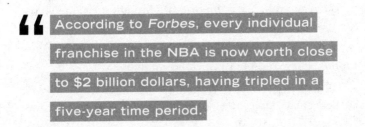

According to *Forbes*, every individual franchise in the NBA is now worth close to $2 billion dollars, having tripled in a five-year time period.

Digital Marketing and Social Media

The tie-in to social media for any business is vital to marketing success today. While it is hard to directly quantify how much revenue is produced from social media engagement, it's clear by the numbers that there is a staggering amount of interaction going on amongst users across the leading social media platforms. According to Statista.com, as of September 2019, the NBA had more than a combined 66 million followers on Facebook and Twitter.[3] This is more than any other sports league. There are also an estimated 28 million followers on Instagram.

Blogger Tony Adrangna provided several key marketing tips used by the NBA. For example, Adragna points to the league providing creative content by several writers on the NBA.com page, with each team also utilizing expert writers to provide game recaps, articles, and more on the team websites. He also points to the league's ability to engage fans with timely content, updated daily, featuring team and the league activities.[4]

As for social media, Adragna writes that, "No other professional sports league does social media as well as the NBA does. Each team employs a social media manager that keeps team social pages fresh with real-time content and updates."[5]

Adragna also makes a point of the benefits of updating social media content very often, keeping your content interesting (so your followers will come back for more), and why interacting with your audience is important. Through social media the NBA uses polls, surveys, and other manners in which to remain interactive with the fans. Plus, the NBA and the franchises use graphics, GIFs, and plenty of video content.

It should also be noted that the NBA's digital online and social media marketing strategy is beyond the on-court action, with photos and articles about what they are doing off the court, such as NBA Cares, Basketball Without Borders, and so forth. The images, videos, articles, and conversations go beyond just sports.

▪ CELEBRITY SIGHTINGS= FREE ENDORSEMENTS

It's difficult to quantify the benefits of celebrity appeal in business but there are frequently celebrities seen at NBA games, and not just in New York and Los Angeles. Considering the cost of celebrity endorsements, or appearances at company events, the free exposure, and enthusiasm, generated by celebrity fans attending NBA games is a major plus, adding to the league's wide visibility and drawing more attention to the league. In fact, celebrity fans have been part of the attraction at NBA games for years. Unlike the grandeur of football or baseball stadiums, the immediacy of an indoor arena with celebrity fans sitting courtside, such as Jack Nicholson at Laker games and Spike Lee at Knicks games adds to the NBA experience. Not unlike a product endorsement, there is a connection between fans and celebrities taking the same couple of hours to watch the same game.

Along with Nicholson and Lee, frequent celebrity attendees at NBA games have included: Drake cheering for the Raptors, Kevin Hart for the 76ers, Jessica Alba for the Warriors, Billy Crystal for the Clippers, Eminem for the Pistons, Matt Damon for the Celtics, Woody Allen for the Knicks, and Beyoncé rooting for the Rockets, among many others.

Celebrity involvement in the NBA goes one giant step further with a number of notable team owners or co-owners which have included: Spanx entrepreneur Sara Blakely, Will Smith and Jada Pinkett Smith, Jay-Z, Justin Timberlake, and Mark Cuban, who has become a TV star with *Shark Tank*. Along with Charlotte's majority owner, Michael Jordon, former NBA stars Grant Hill, Shaq, and Magic Johnson have become minority team owners, or governors, as they are also now called.

A New League

The NBA now has a new league, one in the vastly popular gaming world. This league is based on the game NBA2K which has, with the support of the league, become the foremost video basketball game in the market. The NBA2K series debuted in 1999, but has grown significantly in twenty years to a point in which it now sells roughly ten million copies per year globally.

In a *Forbes* magazine article in early 2019, NBA Commissioner Adam Silver said, "An entire generation of basketball fans engage and connect with NBA teams and players through NBA2K. We are grateful to extend our partnership with Take-Two and the NBPA to build on the enormous popularity of the NBA2K franchise and the continued global growth of basketball."[6]

The game has led to the NBA2K League, a professional competitive gaming league launched by the NBA in conjunction with developer Take-Two in 2018. The state-of-the-gaming-arts league offers top gamers a unique NBA gaming experience, and significant prize money for league champions. As *Forbes* also noted, Adam Silver referred to it as "the NBA's forth league, along with the NBA, WNBA and G League."[7] (Note: The first season saw NBA2K viewers log in over 760,000 hours worldwide.)

The Jr. NBA World Championship

In 2018, the NBA launched the first annual Jr. NBA World Championships. The Jr. NBA basketball program began in 2015 as a free membership program for youth basketball leagues or organizations, such as Boys and Girls Clubs, community centers, YM/YWCAs, YM/YWHAs, Police Athletic Leagues, and so forth. Such leagues or organizations could join online. Grant programs are also available to help teams with expenses.

A global initiative, aptly named World Championships, incorporates much of the world, with teams representing several regions of the United States and teams competing from Africa, Asia Pacific, Canada, China, Europe, the Middle East, India, Latin America, and Mexico. Over 300 youngsters on thirty-two teams from thirty-five countries took part in the first Jr. NBA World Championships, which took place near Orlando, Florida, over the course of a week and included community projects, skills sessions, and a trip to Disney parks. Local competitions have also been added to the undertaking.

Participating coaches in the Jr. NBA are trained and licensed by USA Basketball (U.S.-based coaches) or FIBA (international coaches). In addition, not unlike Basketball Without Borders, which features older players, the tournament is also supported by NBA and WNBA players. Global ambassadors at the 2019 Championships were Dwayne Wade from the NBA and Candace Parker of the WNBA.

While the competition is designed to showcase the best teams, a close watch is kept on the young players. "We developed over the last year with USA Basketball and a group of basketball experts, a set of guidelines and standards that really focused on player health and wellness to really make sure that kids were not playing too often at too young of an age," said

President of Social Responsibility and Player Programs for the NBA Kathy Behrens. "It's also a tournament that is not going to just focus on the on-court competition, but on community programming, and life skills programming," added Behrens.[8]

NBA SWOT Analysis

All of these factors keep the NBA in the public eye, while enhancing league revenue. It is therefore worthwhile to take a closer look at how the league stands today by using a SWOT analysis, which includes the strengths and weakness of the current NBA, along with the opportunities and threats. While strengths and weaknesses of a business are often internal, the threats and opportunities are often external by nature.

League Strengths

▪ Continuous star talent entering the league through scouting at the college and international level allows the NBA to maintain the highest level of competitive professional basketball. Attendance has steadily risen for the league, reaching record numbers in recent years.

▪ The NBA has built, and maintains, a strong, diverse demographic audience ranging from ten to over sixty, with the average age being forty-two. The league also has a strong base of minority and international fans.

▪ The NBA has worked tirelessly to forge deals that allows games to be broadcast in over forty countries which:

Benefits advertisers and sponsors

Enhances worldwide merchandising efforts

Introduces young fans and future players
to the league

- Opening and maintaining league offices in various countries allows the league to make deals abroad and monitor the popularity of the league while keeping a pulse on the growing trends in each nation.
- Community activities and involvement both domestically and internationally connect fans and players through outreach programs such as NBA Cares and NBA Green.
- Youth camps and programs teach young people important skills both on and off the court.
- The league makes tie-ins and connections with pop culture with player and fan activity on social media and player involvement in rap, hip hop, and films. Gaming fans also now have an NBA-sponsored game and league.
- NBA TV provides both NBA and WNBA games plus league-related programming 24/7.
- NBA merchandising continues to be a global multi-billion-dollar industry.
- Corporate sponsorship such as Nike (with whom the league signed a $1 billion-dollar deal which began in 2017–18) continues to increase league revenues.

League Weaknesses

- High ticket prices for major (and some smaller) market teams and the lack of availability of tickets for the average fans. This is due to limited individual game tickets in many markets and a very robust resale of tickets on the secondary market with tickets for teams such as Golden State, the L.A. Lakers, and New York Knicks selling for well-over $500 per seat.
- Player discontent on current teams (i.e. Anthony Davis with New Orleans, Jimmy Butler with Minnesota, etc.) can dissuade fans and disrupt team balance.

- The increasing number of players signing shorter free agent contracts and jumping from team to team impacts team loyalty and TV viewership.

- Younger and millennial fans are moving away from linear broadcasting which is making it more difficult to keep up with fans looking to stream games at their leisure—this has cut into ratings on ESPN and TNT, though not dramatically.

- The NBA's annual All-Star game is dropping in ratings, possibly because of the absurdity of the selection process which leaves no clear demarcation for fans to choose a side to root for (such as east and west).

League Opportunities

- While the game has branched out internationally over the past thirty years, there are still places in Europe, India, and elsewhere in which the league has room to develop a greater fan base.

- With fan interest so high, the league can explore expansion into both new and former markets such as Seattle and St. Louis.

- The NBA can generate potential fan interest for the WNBA by shifting the league's schedule to overlap, somewhat, with the NBA schedule, providing the possibility of double-headers and cross league promotions.

- Exhibition and summer league games could be tied in more closely with NBA Cares and other community events and activities to draw more fans and raise money for charitable activities.

- While the NBA has many outreach projects now, there is always room to expand such much-needed initiatives both domestically and internationally.

League Threats

▪ The biggest threat to a competitive league is becoming unbalanced for any length of time. Too many struggling teams can eventually lose fans' interest and revenue.

▪ The league must continue to monitor who watches games, when they watch them, and where they watch games. Falling behind in digital, streaming technology can be detrimental if the emphasis remains too heavily focused on linear TV.

▪ Doping, drug use, and illegal or violent activities have become issues in the sports world and can be damaging to the league's image should they arise. The NBA needs to remain vigilant in maintaining their anti-doping policies and maintain awareness of other questionable activities of players and league personnel.

▪ Lengthy lockouts due to player and owner discord can be damaging.

▪ Outpricing tickets for the average fans. What is already a problem for many fans can become more serious. The rapidly growing secondary market for tickets is making it difficult for fans to purchase tickets. While ticket bots are illegal as of the Better Online Ticket Sales (BOTS) Act of 2016, the trend continues with ticket brokers buying scores of available tickets. Using BOTs to find the latest NBA player signature sneakers for purchasing and reselling on the secondary market for very high prices has also emerged.

▪ Geo-political factors. Having become a global league the NBA is subject to political incidents that can create controversy and alter or upend relationships with political and/or business leaders in other countries. For example, just prior to the start of the 2019–2020 season,

the NBA found itself in the midst of a controversy regarding the protests against the Chinese government
in Hong Kong. The trouble for the league began when
Rockets GM Daryl Morey tweeted his support for the
protesters, before a preseason game in Tokyo. The
post, which read, "Fight for Freedom, Stand with Hong
Kong." This angered Chinese government officials and
suddenly the league's long-standing positive relationship with China in jeopardy. Despite Morey's apology,
the situation continued to escalate with Yao Ming,
commissioner of the Chinese Basketball Association,
expressing strong dissatisfaction with the GM of the
Rockets, the team he used to play for. The immediate
impact was a ban on NBA televised games in China,
which lasted through the preseason, but was quietly
lifted by the start of the regular season. The NBA does
billions of dollars in business with various nations and
has an incredible following abroad, but politics can
abruptly factor into such relationships.

Clearly the NBA has many strengths, and has been building
on those strengths for years. In the early 1980s, the league
started to gain the traction for which they were laying the foundation for nearly four decades, and David Stern was intent on
capitalizing on that long-anticipated success. Once the league
started on an upward surge, it continued with all thirty franchises enjoying financial success.

The weaknesses are all issues that can be addressed, some of
which cross-over into other sports, such as issues with pricing,
dynamic pricing (which means using supply and demand to
change prices), and doping issues, which means being diligent
and enforcing anti-doping policies. Other issues are just a mat-

ter of staying relevant, which the NBA has been doing with gaming, social media, and working with streaming services. It is important to stay ahead of the curve when it comes to the changing landscape of technology or viewership (on television or another medium).

Opportunities for a successful business, such as the NBA, can be carefully selected based on what the sponsors, owners, and the league believe will enhance the experience for fans. This pertains to inside the arenas and work in the communities, which has unlimited possibilities, especially as the league expands globally.

The two most significant threats to the league are centered around maintaining enough balance in the league to hold fan interest across all thirty franchises, and keeping costs reasonable enough for the average fan to purchase tickets to games. Balance becomes a problem when fans start losing interest in struggling teams. While this has not been a threat in recent years, it would necessitate new ideas to boost and market struggling small market teams should there be teams that are not maintaining their fan base.

The pricing issue is something the league can attack. Since arenas have a lower seating capacity than baseball stadiums, and teams play half the home games, there are fewer tickets and greater demand for those tickets. This may necessitate that the NBA, and individual franchises, take a closer look at the secondary ticket market and seek out ways to curb runaway prices by ticket brokers while shutting down ticket scalpers in areas that have deemed scalping illegal. Like weaknesses, threats to the NBA are manageable with awareness by the league and the franchises.

BUSINESS LESSONS AND OPPORTUNITIES

One of the lessons that David Stern always preached was to learn from those who are doing great things, and not necessarily in your own industry. Therefore, even for those entrepreneurs that are not planning to start a professional sports league, the NBA business methodology can be impactful, stemming from over seventy years of experience and five leaders (commissioners) who took on challenges, sought out applicable solutions, and worked with franchise owners and a strong labor union to create and sustain an extraordinary business.

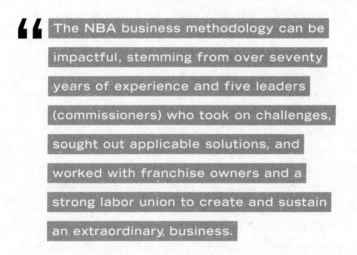

" The NBA business methodology can be impactful, stemming from over seventy years of experience and five leaders (commissioners) who took on challenges, sought out applicable solutions, and worked with franchise owners and a strong labor union to create and sustain an extraordinary business.

Below are five lessons that you can take away from the NBA.

1. *You don't have to reinvent the wheel.* Many of the most success-ful businesses were not the first to break new ground in their industries. For example, Myspace preceded Facebook and Karl Benz (of Mercedes Benz) was selling cars in 1883, years before Ford made them affordable. Likewise, the NBA presented a professional version of a game created in the 1890s and was the culmination of two existing professional basketball leagues, one of which had started in the 1930s.

What Podoloff and the original owners did was combine ex-isting teams with top young talent with other existing teams playing in large venues to get the best of both worlds. They used the basic premise of the game as played in the two prior leagues and adapted rules and made changes as necessary to improve upon the product. By starting with an existing product or service, you can build accordingly, utilizing what works and changing what doesn't until you have created a better product or service that will meet the needs of your intended demo-graphic market. You have an advantage of not having to intro-duce an entirely new product or service to the public. The majority of major businesses have taken an existing concept and improved upon it many times over.

Don't be afraid to innovate. In the early years of the league, the college draft was instituted to provide an immediate means of getting players to smoothly transition into the league with-out losing their fan base from their collegiate careers. The 24-second clock later increased the pace of play, and the three-point shot (which originated in the ABA) added a whole new dimension to the way the game is played.

Being innovative means not being afraid to try new things. Companies have expanded on what they offer for years, such as Lego, a company that grew from a toymaker, featuring attachable plastic bricks, to a multibillion-dollar company selling programmable Lego robots and making feature length motion pictures. Don't rest on the success of a single product or service—keep looking to improve what you offer.

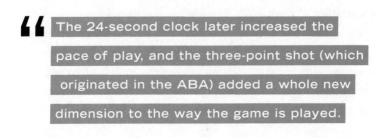

The 24-second clock later increased the pace of play, and the three-point shot (which originated in the ABA) added a whole new dimension to the way the game is played.

2. *Never stop extending your brand.* From a league of seventeen teams, the NBA has expanded to a thirty-team league, encouraging franchise owners to seek out new locations if their current location was not profitable. The expansion of the league westward followed the success of baseball's western expansion and reached untapped markets.

Growth in your business-reach is vital to overall success as you expand your products and services into new markets. This can mean geographical expansion or technical expansion, through your website, or websites, and through social media—or both.

Brand extension means spinning off your current product into various iterations. It often means taking calculated risks, based on studying the marketplace. A broad example comes from the beverage industry where most companies spun off their original product to also sell a diet version of their beverage, a non-caffeinated soft drink, or variations on juices, often combining flavors. NBA spin-offs include the WNBA, the NWBA (National Wheelchair Basketball Association), Jr. NBA,

NBA China, NBA2K, and so on. Each is a version of the same product, the game of basketball.

3. *Utilize brand ambassadors and follow current trends.* The power of brand ambassadors has also been huge for the NBA. While most businesses will not have superstar athletes to promote their brand worldwide, developing and utilizing top performers in your industry, notable product/service users, a community influencer, and/or a spokesperson can be integral when it comes to expanding your brand. Reach out to local or national celebrities to come to your events. Also make an effort to have a presence at community events that attract influencers and/or celebrities.

Have your pulse on the current trends. For example, knowing the latest in fashion can let you know where your logo or company name can appear on what people are wearing. Associate your brand with whatever is tending to your buyers. The NBA players have embraced pop culture on their own volition, with rap songs and movie appearances. The league, however, besides entering the popular gaming market, also made a deal with MGM to tap into the growing popularity of sports gambling with a platform that utilizes real-time data for micro-betting. In short, if it's fashionable, trending, or generating a buzz with your target market explore the possibility of tapping into that new market, or at least having your name/logo visible.

4. *Be community minded, locally and globally.* For years the NBA has utilized community outreach programs to improve education, rebuild neighborhoods, and meet social needs. It's not difficult for any business to reach out to their community, get involved, and make an impact. This goes beyond the bottom

line, and brings a level of social awareness to any business, which is always a positive.

While not every business can have a global impact, most businesses, especially through their reach on the internet, have a global presence, and a global presence means you are expanding your market.

The NBA took steps by opening offices overseas, which helped the league understand the market in other nations, make deals with foreign companies, and grow an interest in basketball in that country. After all, it you are going to market goods and services in another part of the world, you need to know what people want and how to best reach them. For example, beyond the popularity of basketball in China, businesses can tap into the products that are trending by doing ongoing research. For example, American clothing, shoes, sportswear, (including Nike and Adidas sneakers) and vitamins or supplements were all popular products in China as of 2018.

Keep in mind, the key to success overseas is also making sure you establish yourself at home first. The NBA had no intention of going overseas in the 1950s or 1960s while the league was still going through growing pains. Globalization took place once the league was on steady ground and the product was well established. This is true of companies like McDonald's, which was well established in the United States before venturing overseas. Remember to learn about the customs, language nuances, and the culture of global markets so you can best present your product in other parts of the world. In essence you need to "know before you go." Utilize technology to the fullest. When the NBA started, black-and-white television with limited channels was the only option, other than radio. The league embraced technology from the start, landing numerous TV contracts over the years. As long as the product remained strong and sponsors were pleased, the league was in good shape. When ratings dropped, and the league was relegated to tape-delayed games in the 1970s, they worked with the networks to rearrange their season schedules so they would not compete with primetime programming during network sweeps. Over the years, TV deals have become significantly sweeter, in part due to the popularity of the game and in part due to the growing number of networks competing for a piece of the NBA action.

The NBA, however was always aggressive when it came to utilizing the latest technology, signing deals with cable TV—which was growing by leaps and bounds in the late 1970s—and later starting their own network through Turner Broadcasting, NBA TV. As the internet grew, the NBA followed suit with websites, or pages, to support the leagues and each franchise. They furnished bloggers with content and had their own writers working on new content for the site regularly. When social media became all the rage, the league took to Facebook, Twitter, and other platforms. When streaming became the next big thing, the NBA was there.

The point is, with today's diverse media, a successful business needs to stay ahead of the curve and make forays into each new medium that reaches your target audience. Often this necessitates hiring people to devote the time and energy to navigate the latest technology and make sure your business is utilizing it to their advantage. While your company may not warrant your own programming, there are programs, podcasts, and video platforms on which you can market yourself using brand ambassadors, celebrities, business leaders, and/or sponsorship.

Following the trends in media is important when trying to reach your demographic group. For example, millennials watch less linear TV and stream programming more often—they are also likely to listen to a podcast about an issue with which your business aligns. Understand the ways in which your audience best receives their information, and use that medium. The NBA has built an incredible global media presence by always looking for new avenues to explore and then presenting engaging content on each platform or channel.

5. *Deal with adversity with carefully thought-out actions.* The five NBA commissioners share something in common: They have maintained their poise (outwardly) through a number of challenges over the years, while working in conjunction with franchise owners and the NBPA.

Through the years of the ABA, (while concerned about poaching players) they took a "wait and see" approach to the new league, without altering their product and only took legal action when deemed necessary. Owners and players had their disputes, but in the end, they calmly and collectively settled their issues. The same was true of other calamities that shook the league but did not break it.

Maintaining integrity, pride, transparency and an overall strong culture, in which everyone involved wants to be a part of the business, makes it possible to deal with adversity skillfully and productively. Learn from major challenges, make the necessary adjustments, and move forward as the NBA has done for years.

ENDNOTES

Chapter 1

1. Sam Goldpaper, "The First Game," *New York Times*, November 1, 1946. NBA.com, https://nba.com/history/firstgame_feature .html.
2. Eric Nadel, *The Night Wilt Scored 100: Tales From Basketball's Past* (Dallas: Taylor Publishing Company, 1979), 10–12.
3. NBPA. About and History. NBPA.com. https://nbpa.com/about.
4. Robert Bradley, "Labor Pains Nothing New to NBA," ABPR.org, https://apbr.org/labor.html.
5. Robert Bradley.
6. The Association for Professional Basketball Research, www.apbr .org/attendance.html.

Chapter 2

1. The Association for Professional Basketball Research, www.apbr .org/attendance.html.
2. William Johnson, "TV Made It All a New Game," *Sports Illustrated*, December 22, 1969, https://si.com/vault/1969/12/22/618805/ tv-made-it-all-a-new-game.
3. Dick Johnson, "Breaks in the Game," *Newsweek*, June 5, 1967, 66.

Chapter 3

1. Joe Newman, personal interview, July 31, 2019.
2. Joe Newman.
3. Joe Newman.

4. Caselaw.findlaw.com. HAYWOOD v. NATIONAL BASKETBALL ASS'N. Argued: Decided: March 1, 1971, https://caselaw.findlaw.com/us-supreme-court/401/1204.html.

5. Joe Newman, personal interview, July 31, 2019.

6. Joe Newman.

7. Joe Newman.

8. Joe Newman.

9. Terry Pluto, *Loose Balls: The Short, Wild Life of the American Basketball Association* (New York: Simon and Schuster, 2007), 45.

10. Joe Newman, personal interview, July 31, 2019.

11. Joe Newman.

Chapter 4

1. John Papanek, "There's an Ill Wind Blowing for the NBA," *Sports Illustrated*, February 26, 1979, si.com/vault/1979/02/26/823411/theres-an-ill-wind-blowing-for-the-nba-attendance-is-slipping-and-the-leagues-tv-ratings-have-plummeted-leading-to-a-lot-of-cries-and-whispers-about-the-real-problems.

2. John Papanek.

3. Evan Bleier, "The Rivalry That Saved the NBA Began During March Madness: Magic v. Bird," insidehook.com, March 26, 2019, https://insidehook.com/article/sports/the-rivalry-that-saved-the-nba-began-during-march-madness-magic-v-bird.

4. Sam Beidokhti, "The Men Who Saved the NBA," Fadeawayworld.net, March 26, 2017, https://fadeawayworld.net/2017/03/26/the-men-who-saved-the-nba/.

5. Glenn Rifkin, "How the National Basketball Association Put the Bounce Bask in Basketball." Business + Strategy, July 1, 1997, https://strategy-business.com/article/17785?gko=861c4.

6. Glenn Rifkin.

7. Mike Azania, "How David Stern Built The NBA And His Favorite Sports Investments Today," *Forbes SportsMoney*, July 18, 2017, https://forbes.com/sites/mikeozanian/2017/07/18/how-david-stern-built-the-modern-nba-and-his-favorite-sports-investments-today/#574109385da7.

Chapter 5

1. Joanne Lannin, personal interview, July 19, 2019.

2. Joanne Lannin.

3. Lyndsey D'Arcangelo, "The WNBA's Problem Isn't Lack of Interest From Men. It's Women," HuffPost, March 15, 2017, https://huffpost.com/entry/the-wnbas-biggest-problem_b_9437480.

4. Joanne Lannin, personal interview, July 19, 2019.

5. Joanne Lannin.

6. Brigitte Yuille, "Top WNBA Salaries: How do They Stack Up?" Investopia.com, May 17, 2019, https://www.investopedia.com/financial-edge/0410/top-wnba-salaries.aspx.

7. Joanne Lannin, "In Its 20th Season, Is the WNBA Where It Should Be? Finding a Way to Play, May 2, 2017, https://findingawaytoplay.com/2016/05/11/in-its-20th-season-is-the-wnba-where-it-should-be/.

8. Lindsey Horsting, "L.A.'s Tiffany Jackson-Jones Is The Definition of Role Model," WNBA.com, August 25, 2017, https://www.wnba.com/news/l-s-tiffany-jackson-jones-definition-role-model/.

9. Lindsey Horsting.

10. Olivia Abrams, "New WNBA Commissioner Cathy Engelbert Has an Unconventional Background and an Unusually Tall Order," *Forbes*, July 17, 2019, https://forbes.com/sites/oliviaabrams/2019/07/17/wnba-commissioner-cathy-engelbert/#7173c7fa2de8.

11. Olivia Abrams.

Chapter 6

1. Tim Reynolds, "'Our Fans Are Everywhere': NBA Still Growing Internationally," APnews.com, October 12, 2018, https://apnews.com/2397a39e69ce418ba2e13716b5dee1e9.

2. Tim Reynolds.

3. Kim Bohuny, personal interview, September 26, 2019.

4. Kim Bohuny.

5. Andrew Sharp, "Coming to America," *Sports Illustrated*, 2018, https://si.com/longform/2018/nba-international-oral-history/index.html.

6. Glenn Rifkin, "How the National Basketball Association Put the Bounce in Basketball," strategy-business.com. July 1, 1997, https://strategy-business.com/article/17785?gko=861c4.

7. CVC Digital Archives, "The NBA Is Coming to Toronto," cbc.ca, November 14, 1993, www.cbc.ca/archives/entry/the-nba-is-coming-to-toronto.

8. Michael Lore, "Yao Ming's Impact on the Growth of NBA and Basketball in China," Culture Trip, October 10, 2017, https://theculturetrip.com/asia/china/articles/yao-mings-impact-on-the-growth-of-nba-and-basketball-in-china/.

9. Kim Bohuny, personal interview, September 26, 2019.

10. Kim Bohuny.

11. Kim Bohuny.

12. Kim Bohuny.

Chapter 7

1. Jefferson Morley, "Fans May Be Locking Out Professional Basketball," *Washington Post*, November 14, 1998, https://www.washingtonpost.com/archive/local/1998/11/14/fans-may-be-locking-out-professional-basketball/4659031e-4d8c-40ce-8eca-d3cb927fd6a6/.

2. Dave Hollander, "What if the NBA Had a Black Commissioner in 1981?" Huffington Post, May 29, 2014. Reprinted from "The Best of All Worlds for a Black Pro," *Ebony*, January 1975, https://huffpost.com/entry/what-if-the-nba-had-a-bla_b_5413414.

3. Thomas Golianopoulos, "It Was All about Money: An Oral History of the 1998–1999 NBA Lockout," TheRinger.com, February 14, 2019, https://theringer.com/nba/2019/2/14/18222040/lockout-1998-99-season-david-stern-david-falk-billy-hunter-patrick-ewing-michael-jordan-oral-history.

4. Thomas Golianopoulos.

5. Paul D. Staudohar. "Labor Relations in Basketball: The Lockout of 1998–99," Monthly Labor Review, April 1999, https://bls.gov/mlr/1999/04/art1full.pdf.

6. Paul D. Staudohar.

7. Thomas Golianopoulos, "It Was All about Money: An Oral History of the 1998–1999 NBA Lockout," TheRinger.com, February 14, 2019, https://theringer.com/nba/2019/2/14/18222040

/lockout-1998-99-season-david-stern-david-falk-billy-hunter-patrick-ewing-michael-jordan-oral-history.

Chapter 8

1. J. D. Adande, "Why Kobe Was So Important to the NBA," ESPN.com, November 30, 2015, https://espn.com/nba/story/_/id/14256934/why-kobe-bryant-was-important-nba.
2. Selena Hill, "The 5 Cities That Would Benefit the Most by the 'LeBron Effect,'" Blackenterprise.com, July 2, 2018, https://blackenterprise.com/economic-impact-lebron-james/.
3. Brad Adgate, "Why The 2017–18 Season Was Great For The NBA." *Forbes*, April 25, 2018, https://forbes.com/sites/bradadgate/2018/04/25/the-2017-18-season-was-great-for-the-nba/#767e14b92ecb.
4. SI Wire, "NBA announces 9-year TV deal with ESPN, Turner Sports," SI.com, October 5, 2014, https://si.com/nba/2014/10/05/new-nba-tv-deal-worth-24-billion.
5. Bob Foltman, "Stern Responds to Wild Brawl: Repulsive," *Chicago Tribune*, November 21, 2004, https://chicagotribune.com/news/ct-xpm-2004-11-21-0411210490-story.html.
6. Mike Pravda, "NBA Lockout Ends: A Comprehensive Timeline From Five Wild Months," SBnation.com, November 28, 2011, https://sbnation.com/nba/2011/11/28/2588568/nba-lockout-2011-timeline-david-stern.
7. Liz Robbins, "A Somber Stern Surveys the Damage to the NBA," *New York Times*, July 25, 2007, https://www.nytimes.com/2007/07/25/sports/basketball/25nba.html.

Conclusion

1. Kurt Badenhausen and Mike Ozanian, "NBA Team Values: Knicks On Top At $4 Billion," *Forbes*, February 6, 2019, https://forbes.com/sites/kurtbadenhausen/2019/02/06/nba-team-values-2019-knicks-on-top-at-4-billion/#1e4210cae667.
2. Nathan Reiff, "How the NBA Makes Money," Investopedia.com, September 24, 2019, https://investopedia.com/articles/personal-finance/071415/how-nba-makes-money.asp.
3. Statista.com, "Content Market Trend Study 2019," https://statista.com/statistics/322941/facebook-fans-twitter-followers-of-nba/.

4. Tony Adranga, "How Your Brand Can Use the NBA's Brilliant Digital Marketing Strategy," Primitivesocial.com, October 26, 2018, https://primitivesocial.com/blog/author/tony-adragna/page/5.
5. Tony Adranga.
6. Brian Mazique, "NBA 2K And The NBA's Massive Extension: What It Could Mean For The Future,"*Forbes*, January 15, 2019, https://forbes.com/sites/brianmazique/2019/01/15/nba-2k-and-the-nbas-massive-extension-what-it-could-mean-for-the-future/#d562a962ccd1.
7. Brian Mazique.
8. Brian Martin, "NBA Extends Global Youth Basketball Initiative with New Global Competition," NBA.com, December 18, 2017, https://nba.com/article/2017/12/18/nba-expands-youth-basketball-initiative-new-global-competition.

INDEX

THE
CAPITAL
ONE
STORY

Available now from HarperCollins Leadership

I t's impossible to go a day without seeing or hearing mention of Capital One. Their witty, star-studded commercials and print ads are ubiquitous. Though relatively new to the banking and credit industry compared to their historic competitors, they have been steadily growing and edging out the competition for the past twenty-five years. They're growing so much they are now one of the top 10 credit issuers, keeping company with some of the most enduring banks in U.S. history. Capital One is not just enduring but historic and groundbreaking as well. It's hard to imagine that such a new company could have anything in common with the legacy banks, but in fact, they do.

A Very Brief History of U.S. Banking and Lending

Some names are synonymous with banking—BNY Mellon and JP Morgan Chase for example. Some with history. Some are synonymous with both. Enjoying a resurge in popularity thanks in large part to the smash hit *Hamilton*, founding fathers Aaron Burr and Alexander Hamilton are some such names. Though the two are well-known frenemies and helped shape our nation, what is little known, however, is that the two rivals are also the founders of two of the largest and longest-enduring U.S. banks. While we tend to think of "Big Banks" as something unique to our age, they have been part of the fabric of American life since its inception.

It's All About the Hamiltons

One of the U.S.'s oldest banks, The Bank of New York, was founded by none other than Alexander Hamilton himself in 1784. Upon his return from serving in Congress, Hamilton returned to New York and saw a business opportunity—credit. Merchants in the growing city needed access to credit in order to finance their new business ventures. However, there was one segment of the business population Hamilton refused to lend to—his enemies, the Jeffersonian Republicans—which essentially amounted to half of the merchants in New York.

Enter Hamilton's long-time rival, Aaron Burr. Not to be outdone, Aaron Burr, who had been outspokenly anti-Federalist and anti-credit, in a bold (and some might even argue devious) move reworded some language in a charter that had been created to build a private water company for New Yorkers. In the newly worded charter, Burr made a provision that the water company could accept deposits and make loans. In essence the Manhattan Water Co. was a bank—or what became known as the Manhattan Bank. Burr could now lend to his peers who had been shut out previously by Hamilton and his Federalist friends. With this new influx in money and access, the entire political and financial landscape changed in America.

Some historians, like Robert E. Wright, author of *One Nation Under Debt: Hamilton, Jefferson, and the History of What We Owe,* argues it's the reason Jefferson was even elected president in 1800.[1] With the new infusion of cash flow, he had access to otherwise inaccessible funds thanks to Burr's Manhattan Bank. Money playing a role in politics, it appears, is as old as America itself. Similarly, shutting people out of credit and discriminating against them (and finding ways to bypass discrimination) has been as well.

Though the times have certainly changed, banking and the rivalries among banks have remained largely the same. Hamilton's Bank of New York still survives today, though it is known as New York Mellon (BNY having merged with Mellon in 2006). Similarly, Burr's Manhattan bank survives as JPMorgan Chase, (having first merged with Chase and then JPMorgan in 2000). To this day, our founding fathers' banks, JPMorgan Chase and Mellon endure and are on the Top 10 list of largest banks in the U.S.[2] In fact, nine out of the ten largest banks in the U.S. have been around for more than 100 years. They have survived forty-seven recessions,[3] stock market crashes, an ensuing Depression, Democratic and Republican presidencies, a Civil War, two World Wars, countless other wars, mergers, acquisitions, and even Ponzi schemes. These old banks and the leaders that founded them, have been, for better or for worse, part of the continuing unfolding American story.

Capital One's Origin Story

Among these top ten largest U.S. banks (by assets), however, one bank stands out precisely because it *hasn't* shared in this rich and complex past. Though it is only twenty-five years old, Capital One is no less a part of the ever unfolding American story—and more accurately—its future. Its origin story, ironically, comes about for reasons very similar to why the two oldest and largest began in the first place: The consumers' need for access to credit and the founders of the bank's desire to bypass discrimination.

Capital One, though fairly new, is linked intrinsically to both American spirit and history. Its founders also share many striking similarities to U.S. banking's early founders. Fairbank, like Burr, is American-born, and Morris, like Hamilton, is an immigrant. When they founded Capital One, the two were young visionaries who saw consumer needs changing and were ready to seize the opportunity. Like Burr, they saw that only half of all Americans at the time had access to credit and they sought to democratize the process. Like Hamilton, they wanted to bring America into a modern era, where it could both prosper and grow and meet the demands of a changing socioeconomic, political, and rapidly developing landscape. But, unlike Burr and Hamilton, the two won't be meeting in a duel on a field in New Jersey anytime soon. To this day, they remain friends and leaders and in the banking and FinTech (the area of where financial services and digital technology meet) industries. Unlike any other large bank on the Top Ten List, Capital One's founder still sits in the CEO chair and commands the vision of the bank itself.

Banking Reimagined

In the past two decades, Capital One has enjoyed not just a meteoric rise in the financial industry, but in U.S. business as a whole, specifically in the FinTech industry. From its start, Capital One has been shaking up the old, storied banking industry and brought new and innovative practices that have changed how people bank and understand their relationship with what was in their wallet. Robert Alexander, Capital One's CIO, who has served in various capacities over his 20-year tenure with the company is well aware of advantages of being the relative new kid on the block. One of the key advantages is having a mindset focused on innovation and technology from the outset. "Our products are just ephemeral products. It is principally software and data. Yes, we have branches, and yes, we have pieces of plastic that you put in your wallet today, though some people just carry them on their phone as digital versions of that. Our products though are intangible products, and so at the core of our business is the important role that technology plays, and it is about software, and it is about data and analytics, and it is about how you bring all of that together to create a great experience for customers."[4]

Alexander, and by extension, Capital One as a bank, recognize this is where the financial world is going and has been going for the past two decades. Gone are the days of safe deposit boxes, ledgers, and, in some cases, bank tellers or even ATMs. Instead, Capital One's primary focus has been on a digital strategic realization. Alexander credits this vision to Fairbank. "Our whole executive team is aligned around this view that we need to be technology leaders and digital leaders in our industry to win," Alexander says. And by win he means become the leader in *almost every segment* in banking, not just credit cards. Though Capital One started as a monoline credit card company—with no savings accounts, no checking accounts, no safe deposit boxes or branches, it is currently active in numerous segments of commercial banking. "We have a mix of products and a mix of customers that are more slanted toward digital than other large financial institutions. We are one of a short list of institutions that have a national footprint, so that we can build a national brand on the back of a credit card, on the back of our digital bank, as well as other businesses. We have a great positioning strategically on multiple dimensions," Alexander continues.[5]

The strategy Alexander speaks of dates back to the start of the bank itself. Morris and Fairbank met while working at a consultancy firm. Fairbank hired Morris just out of business school. Some of their assignments at the firm required that they work with historic, large New York banking institutions. While working with a legacy bank, Fairbank began to see patterns—the most profitable parts of the banks were their credit card lines, and yet no one seemed to be paying attention to them. Rather, the bankers' focus was on investments or other financial services. No one was looking at the data, and the data was telling both Morris and Fairbank that credit was both profitable, and an untapped market. At the time only 55 percent of Americans had access to credit.[6] Determined to change how banks do business and help consumers have access to credit, Fairbank, with the help of his friend Morris, ultimately transformed the modern banking industry that had withstood the winds of change for more than two-hundred years.

United by their vision for a new kind of banking and determined to bring banking into the 20th and then 21st centuries based on real data, Morris and Fairbank launched a new type of bank in 1994 and with it a new way for Americans to engage in business, trade, build credit, create wealth, and ultimately, as the nation's founders intended, pursue happiness.

What to Expect in This Book

In this book you will find out how Fairbank took his vision for a new kind of banking and created a different kind of bank, a "fair bank" if you will, one that America had not seen before. You will learn how he and Morris overcame early obstacles, both personal and professional, and how they eventually disrupted a historic and slow-to-change, Big-Bank dominated industry and you'll learn the tactics they used to quickly dominate the market. You'll learn how they were one of the first banks in the world to use consumer data and research to look for trends in the marketplace. You'll also find out how they dealt with pitfalls and major challenges, like the subprime mortgage crisis and the crash of 2008. Every young company has to learn to withstand the inevitable learning curves and growing pains—and Capital One did so and is still standing. They dealt with internal and external turmoil, politics, and the changing landscape of banking—especially as it related to online banking and ongoing technological innovations.

Over the past decade Capital One has enjoyed enormous growth—building its headquarters in McLean, Virginia, and creating a company culture and environment that many have regarded as one of the best in the world. In fact, *Fortune* magazine named Capital One to its "100 Best Companies to Work For" list.[7] As Capital One has grown, they have focused not just on their own bottom line but on the bottom line of their customers and raising spending and consumer awareness, launching a budgeting app for consumers, called ENO in 2019. In their drive to change how people relate to their own money and where it is kept, Capital One has launched a "This is Banking Reimagined" campaign and has created banking cafes in partnership with Peet's Coffee, inviting places where people can bank, plan their financial future with a money coach, engage with community, and enjoy a cup of coffee.

But perhaps its most controversial move has been to the cloud. While adapting to a rapidly changing banking market, Capital One has taken advantage of advances in FinTech, core banking, D2C retail customer apps and moved away from legacy systems (in-house developed banking software). They have now begun to operate on the cloud, making their bank more agile, versatile, fast, and infinitely scalable. In doing so, they have faced scrutiny for such a move, and it was called into further question after a hack exposed millions of consumers' data in late July 2019. Though the hack was not caused by the cloud server, but an individual employed at Amazon Web Services, the cloud provider, Capital One is no less dealing with the fallout of a common potential threat to all American businesses. You'll find out here how they dealt with the security breach, how they ensure the integrity and safety of their data, and the ongoing innovation and steps they are taking to mitigate these risks in the future.

Ultimately, you'll learn how two men with a vision and unique approach to data-driven marketing built a new kind of bank. You'll understand the inner workings of the bank and the consumer credit industry, how banking is being reimagined constantly, and just how important our financial institutions are not just to our past and present, but our future as well.

The future is within reach.

When you start making your goals a top priority, everything falls into place. Learn from the leaders inspiring millions & apply their strategies to your professional journey.

Leadership Essentials Blog

Activate 180 Podcast

Interactive E-courses

Free templates

LEADERSHIP
ESSENTIALS
by HarperCollins Leadership

For more business and leadership advice and resources, visit hcleadershipessentials.com.